How to
BE HEALED
and Stay Healed

Divine power
for your mind
and body

ALISS CRESSWELL

How To Be Healed and Stay Healed

© Copyright 2018 – Aliss Cresswell

All Scripture quotations are taken from the
New International Version © 1973, 1978, 1984
by International Bible Society unless otherwise stated.

Disclaimer: The information contained in this book is for educational and instructional purposes only and is not intended as medical, legal or ethical advice or opinion. This book is not intended as a substitute for the medical advice of physicians.

ISBN 13: 9780957264243
ISBN 10: 0957264240

Published by FiftyFive Eleven Ltd

Printed in the USA

More information and resources:
www.AlissCresswell.com

About the Author

Aliss Cresswell is well known for releasing miracles of breakthrough and demonstrating God's love and power everywhere she goes. With her 'miracle café' and gift shops in England attracting worldwide attention, she now travels with her husband Rob offering powerful Spirit Lifestyle® training and resources and launching others into a life of miracles. Rob and Aliss have been married for over thirty years and have two adult children and a grandson.

For more details visit
www.AlissCresswell.com
www.FaceBook.com/AlissCresswell

Other books by Aliss Cresswell:

A Diary of Miracles (part 1)

A Diary of Miracles (part 2)

The Normal Supernatural Christian Life

Books by Rob Cresswell:

The Believer's Guide to Survival

The Threefold Miracle Mandate

Contents

Introduction

A man shared with me how his wife had read my book, 'The Normal Supernatural Christian Life' and how she had been encouraging him to read it. He wasn't interested until one day his wife left it by the bed, she went out and then he went downstairs. There was the book in the living room which freaked him out, so he went into another room and that same copy showed up there too. He reckoned he may as well read it, and as he picked up the book, the power of the Holy Spirit almost knocked him over, so he lay on the sofa and read it from cover to cover. He felt the power of God go through him and he told me he has never been the same since!

Another time, I was in our neighborhood of Blacon, Chester with a young woman who had just encountered the power of Jesus for the first time. She asked me for a Bible. I picked up a copy that the Gideons had given us and handed it to her. She looked shocked and threw it back at me! But she obviously wanted it, so I handed it to her again. She did exactly the same thing. She blurted out that the Bible was vibrating in her hands and she was so surprized, she quickly passed it back to me again. This is the power I'm talking about. This is the power of God and it is available to you right now to transform your body, your soul and your life.

Keep reading and in Chapter One I will release that power for you personally.

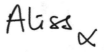

CHAPTER ONE

Divine Power Released for You

Let's begin with a miracle so I can demonstrate the divine power available to you. In fact, when you picked up this book you may already have experienced an unusual feeling of electricity or tingling or peace or excitement or you may have seen a bright light or beautiful colors. Get used to experiencing those things as you become more aware of the Kingdom of Heaven whilst reading this book.

I'm going to share a true story with you of a woman who was miraculously healed of Parkinson's Disease. And whilst you're reading about this woman, receive healing into your body at the same time.

A few years back, I was the 'after dinner speaker' at a hotel in Wales. I shared some supernatural stories of amazing things that I'd witnessed - people being healed, evil spirits leaving, financial miracles, angelic visitations and lives transformed. I was inviting dinner guests to come to the front and experience the same power in their own lives, when a woman came out pushing a lady in a wheelchair. She'd brought her friend along who had Parkinson's Disease and been confined to a wheelchair for many years.

I could see that the woman was hunched over; she was thin, with greying skin and a dullness in her eyes. Her voice was so quiet I could hardly hear her and I could see by her thin body that her muscles must have atrophied. However, this poor woman in the wheelchair lifted her head slightly and mouthed some words to me, not much more than a whisper. I had to crouch down and put my ear to her mouth to try and understand what she was saying. She said, "I want to be healed."

I laid my hand gently on her shoulder and I invited the divine presence of Jesus and the power of the Holy Spirit to come. I told Parkinson's Disease to leave, all the symptoms to go and I released the healing power of Jesus into her body. She lifted up her head and began to mouth more words. I bent down and could faintly hear, "I want to walk." I took a deep breath, and then told those nearby that she was about to have a go at walking. They all looked anxiously at one another, but between us we moved the foot rests of her wheelchair out of the way. With her friend on one side and me on the other, we helped the woman move forward to the edge of her wheelchair.

She began to lean on my arm to push herself up, so between her friend and myself, we helped her stand up. I could see tears in her friend's eyes begin to tumble down her cheeks and with her heart in her mouth, she and I watched as the woman stood up straight for a few seconds, lifted one foot and then the next and proceeded to walk. I'll never forget that moment – everyone in that grand hotel ballroom was cheering and clapping as the woman not only did a lap around the room unaided, but she pushed her own wheelchair all the way to the car outside and jumped into the vehicle without help.

The same power that enabled that woman to be completely healed of an incurable disease and remain healed, is available to you too. And you don't have to go anywhere or meet a 'special' person or pay lots of money to receive that healing power for yourself. That power is working right now and as you read this book you'll find out where that power comes from, why you can receive it, how to stay healed and how to share it with others. But first, I'm going to release some of that miracle working power into your life right now.

So here goes. I love doing miracles – I love to see the look on the person's face as I release divine power into their life and something dramatic happens that changes them forever and brings them hope and peace and joy. I know I'm not there with you physically, but I want to help transform your life and your quality of life, and the power of the Holy Spirit is available for you wherever you are. Jesus said, "I came to bring you life and life in all its fulness". Is that what you want? Are you ready to receive a free gift from God right now? It's His power. He is the Life: I am just a vessel that He uses.

There is an anointing (that's a Biblical word for spiritual power symbolized by oil dripping) from the Holy Spirit right now for you: all you need to do is receive it.

Perhaps you could put your hands out in front of you with palms upwards as though you are about to receive a gift. You could say, "Come and fill me Holy Spirit with your power. Fill me Jesus with your healing presence." Take a deep breath in of the Holy Spirit. And then breathe out all the stress, anxiety and darkness associated with the illness or pain in your body and mind.

Breathe in the Holy Spirit again, inhale deeply and invite the 'Prince of Peace' to walk into your body, your mind and your emotions. Breathe out everything that is contrary to your peace, your healing and your joy.

As I write this I sense the tangible presence of Jesus and I release His powerful healing presence to you right now as you read this book. I tell all pain to go now in Jesus' name. Why not breathe in the Holy Spirit again and breathe out all the pain, trauma, sadness, worry and anxiety?

Now think about what is happening in your body. You may begin to feel heat, tingling, euphoria, lightness or simply a sense of peace. Even if you can't feel anything, something is happening to you already. If you were in pain, check if the pain or any other symptom is still there or diminishing. You may already be healed but whether you have full healing or not yet, keep reading as what I'm about to tell you in this book could alter the course of your life completely. It has the potential to bring healing and wholeness to you and your loved ones and also to everyone you meet.

CHAPTER TWO

Where Does Sickness Come From?

I n the beginning God created the galaxies, the universe and our world. The Bible says He made everything good. He created men and women who would live forever and be His children. He loved them and gave them authority to rule over the earth (Genesis 1:28). There was no death, no sin, no disease, no war nor famine. God loves His children and He wanted them to love Him too and have a special, perfect relationship with Him. He gave them free will so they could choose to love Him. Love is not truly love unless it is given freely, so God gave them a choice that would enable them to trust Him; He said they could eat the fruit of any tree in the Garden of Eden except one, the tree of the knowledge of good and evil.

Why bad things happen in this world

Satan had been cast out of heaven to earth for trying to take God's throne. When he saw God's beautiful creation and beloved creatures he seized an opportunity to take revenge. In the form of a serpent,

Satan persuaded the man and woman to trust his word instead of God's word. Adam and Eve disobeyed God by eating the fruit of the forbidden tree. This was a catastrophic mistake. They had now, in effect, handed the keys of authority over the earth to satan. Since that time, sin, death and disease have reigned in our world because of man's disobedience to God. We are all born into a fallen world, under the power of satan and deserving of the penalty of death. The Bible says that satan comes to "steal, kill and destroy"; most of us have experienced this in our lives! But the Bible also says that Jesus came to destroy the work of satan and to give us life to the full (see John 10:10).

I come across many people suffering pain and debilitating conditions who don't need to be. They don't realize that when they accept the problem, they are in fact coming into agreement with the enemy's plan for their lives. But because of what Jesus accomplished on the cross, they don't have to put up with the pain or condition any longer. Beth was one of these people until I met her last year and she discovered the truth. Here she describes what happened:

"I was on my knees cleaning the shower floor and as I stood up, my back twisted. I felt spasms and severe pain in my lower back. Over the next few days and weeks the pain continued and I knew something was seriously wrong. I spent most of the next year in bed or on the couch in debilitating pain, even crawling to get from place to place to

16

avoid stress on my lower back. This event changed my life and I found myself crying out to God daily for healing. I had visited my doctor as well as specialists and was given six epidurals and pain medication to cope with the pain until they could figure out what was going on.

My life had quickly become one of "I can't do this" or "I can't do that" because of the pain. After many X-rays, MRI scans and specialists, I was diagnosed with bulging discs in the spine between L4 and L5 and was told I needed surgery. I know now that I came into agreement with the pain and disfunction of my spine. I never lost hope that I would someday be healed but had no idea that all the while, I was coming into agreement with the enemy with this condition. Precious time was lost throughout my children's teenage years due to me not being able to feel anything but pain. I know now that the devil had me right where he wanted me; defeated and crippled.

Over the next few years things went from bad to worse. I was diagnosed with an auto immune disease, and then out of the blue my appendix suddenly became septic and ruptured while visiting family in another State and I was rushed into emergency surgery which thankfully saved my life. If all this wasn't enough, I was then diagnosed with breast cancer two years ago and was told it had spread. However, the Lord began to show me a better way than the treatment plan I was offered. Then I met Aliss and Rob Cresswell last year and I learned about healing through the power of Jesus and discovered that I had been coming into agreement with satan's plan for my life instead of God's good plan.

My life has dramatically changed. The cancer has gone. Then an interesting thing happened a few months back which helped me understand what was going on in the spirit realm. I had been told by doctors that I had permanent nerve damage in my back and legs and would need to remain on my prescription of 1800mg of Gabapentin a day just to get by. I was helping Rob and Aliss the morning of one of their supernatural workshops. The pain did something I hadn't noticed before. All of a sudden, the pain went to a debilitating level and I was unable to even walk without crying. The timing of the pain right before doing ministry made me stop and consider that maybe it really was an evil spirit causing the problem.

The following day, I was telling Aliss about the pain and what had happened the previous morning. She calmly looked at me with a smile and said there was nothing wrong with me - it was just a demon, a spirit of infirmity and a spirit of pain lying to me. She asked if I would like to get rid of it? Of course, I said yes! I waited for her to do something, but she told me to tell it to go, so I did. I told the demon to leave, I made it clear it couldn't stay and told it to go to the foot of Jesus where He would deal with it! I immediately noticed the pain leaving.

Aliss instructed me to jump up from the chair I was sitting on. I laughed and said I couldn't do that, but she insisted, so I did. I stood up quickly and began to walk. I was amazed at how much better I felt; I could hardly believe it. Each day I began to walk more and the pain went completely. I now know that I came into agreement with the devil. I gradually reduced my medication and can say with joyful tears in my eyes that I am completely free of all medication and the demon that had attached itself to my nerves is now gone. I am free to do what the Lord has called me to do for the first time in many years! I will be forever grateful and thankful to Aliss for her faithfulness in carrying out God's plan for her life so that we can walk in the freedom that Jesus intended."

Beth was able to be healed and set free through the power of Jesus. You can be healed and set free too. Jesus has made it possible through His death and resurrection. He has overcome all the power of the enemy and the power of Jesus is available to you right now.

God's plan for your life

Because He loves you so much, God sent His only Son, Jesus into the world to be born and live as a man. He had no sin because He was born of God and He lived a sinless life, but He chose to die on the cross and take all the punishment for our sin and disease. 750 years before Jesus came to earth, a prophet named Isaiah wrote this about Jesus going to the cross: "He took up our sicknesses, weaknesses and distresses and carried our sorrows and pains… He was pierced for our transgressions, He was crushed for our guilt and iniquities; the punishment that brought us peace was upon Him, and by His wounds we are healed and made whole" (see Isaiah 53).

Before Jesus was crucified He said to His followers, "I will give you the keys of the Kingdom of Heaven" (Matthew 16:19). The Bible says that when Jesus died He went into hell and took back the keys of authority over this world from satan. He made a public spectacle of satan and overcame him once and for all! (Colossians 2:13-15). Then Jesus was raised to life from the dead, having defeated death, sin, sickness and all the powers of darkness. He gives to every person who follows Him the keys of authority over the earth and over all the power of satan (Luke 10:19).

"For I know the plans I have for you, declares the Lord, plans to prosper you and not to harm you, plans to give you hope and a future" (Jeremiah 29:11).

Forgiveness from sin and freedom from guilt

The Bible says that "all have sinned and fall short of the glory of God" (Romans 3:23). Sin means missing the mark. Many of us carry around guilt and shame from the things we have done in the past. Even the best person in the world has missed the mark. Many people try to reach God by being a good person or doing religious duties. But that is not enough.

"For God so loved the world (that's you and me) that He gave His only Son, that whoever believes in Him shall not perish but will have eternal life." (John 3:16).

Jesus said that He is *the* way to God. "I am the way, the truth and the life. No one comes to the

Father, except through me" (John 14:6). The only way to God is through Jesus.

Jesus had no sin, but He paid the price for our sin. He took the punishment that we deserve when He died on the cross. He rose again, victorious. "I am the Living One; I was dead, and look, I am alive for ever and ever. And I hold the keys of death and hell" (Revelation 1:18). He conquered satan and all the powers of darkness. Jesus has the keys of authority over all the earth.

This means that instead of having to live in the Kingdom of darkness, being subject to fear, sin, disease, addictions, pain, torment and hopelessness, we can now be free from these things and live in the Kingdom of light, the Kingdom of God, here on earth. "Everyone who believes in Him (that is, Jesus) is freed from all guilt and declared right with God" (Acts 13:39).

Let's thank Him for what He has done. Why not say this with me?:

"Thank you, Jesus that you made it possible for me to be set free from sin, sickness and death. Thank you, Father God that you love me so much you sent your beloved son Jesus to die in my place. Thank you, Jesus for doing this for me. I ask you to make yourself known to me in a new way. Please reveal the truth to me about what you accomplished on the cross and how much you love me."

CHAPTER THREE

Does God Want You Well?

*"...know the truth, and the truth
will set you free." John 8:32*

You may simply not have known the truth about healing until now and therefore not realized you can be healed straight away. We have seen so many people dramatically healed by Jesus that my diaries documenting some of those miracles have been published and have been read by thousands of people around the world. Here's just one of the miracles and this is taken from my book, 'A Diary of Miracles Part I':

"Thursday 2nd July

Just before we closed up our café for the day, a lady brought in her neighbor for prayer for healing. She was in a wheelchair suffering from multiple sclerosis. I was busy clearing up but managed to chat with her briefly. She said she'd had MS for 24 years and had been in the wheelchair for the past seven years as her health had deteriorated. She was in a lot of pain and couldn't move from the waist down. She told me that she didn't believe it is God's will to heal her, but she knows Jesus. We quickly showed her some scriptures such as Psalm 103:3,4, "Forget not all His benefits; He forgives all our sins and heals all our diseases" and "By His wounds we are healed," Isaiah 53. We said a quick prayer asking God to heal her fingers of MS as a sign that he wants to heal her (I remembered my friend's fingers were healed of MS first) and that He'd heal her over the weekend.

Saturday 4th July

Arrived back home very tired (from Blacon Festival) and there was a message on our voicemail from the lady who'd brought her friend into the café with MS on Thursday. Called her back and she told me some amazing news. Her neighbor had gone home on Thursday after we'd prayed for her and read her the Scriptures. Usually before going to sleep she would pray and ask God to give her the strength to get through each day. That night she said, "God, please heal me." She woke up yesterday and realized that her bent finger was straight! Today she called her friend and asked her to go round. Apparently all the pain had left her body and her legs no longer felt heavy. Her friend asked if she'd tried to get up, but she hadn't. So at her suggestion, she had a go at standing up. Apparently in the past it would take a couple of people to lift her out of the wheelchair with difficulty. This time she just stood up on her own without any help! She said her legs felt really light. Her feet aren't moving yet but she can stand up and sit down unaided and that is a major miracle. Normally it takes four or five goes to get her into bed. Last night she got into bed straight away and turned over during the night! Also she's not dizzy any more. Hallelujah! Complete healing Lord. She said she's coming back into the café next week. I can't wait to see her. I can hardly believe it. Wow. Lord, you are so wonderful. I can't stop crying!

Thursday 9 July

The lady with MS came in again today. She was in her wheelchair, so I wondered if she was still healed. I hardly dare ask, but she showed me what she could do. She just got up easily and quickly on her own from her wheelchair! Her face was beaming. She looked so different. She said the pain hadn't come back. As she was standing I asked if she'd tried to walk. She said she hadn't and looked worried. I suggested we move her wheelchair and see if she could move her feet. We said we'd hold onto her and not let her fall. The people at the other tables were all watching wide-eyed. We held onto her as she attempted to turn sideways so she could walk forwards. She managed to do that OK. Then, after 24 years of not walking and not using the muscles in her legs, she slowly and gently lifted one foot and placed it in front, then the other, then she let go of us and began to walk unaided. We couldn't believe it. She walked all the way to the other side of the café, turned around and walked back on her own. Then she sat on a wooden chair and stayed there chatting, with tears rolling down her cheeks for at least an hour! She said not only are her legs light, but so is her heart. She said her relationship with Jesus is much closer now."

This lovely woman was healed by Jesus just as soon as she heard the Scriptures making it clear that God's will was to heal her. All she needed to do was to receive and believe. The same applies to you.

If you want to be healed through divine power, the highest power in the Universe which is through God, then it's important to understand if it's God's will for you to be healed personally. We've discussed how Jesus has made it possible for you to be healed, but now let's discover if it is in fact His will for you to be well.

One of my favourite verses in the Bible is "Praise the Lord, O my soul, and forget not all His benefits, who forgives all your sins and heals all your diseases" (Psalm 103:2,3). The message is clear: God forgives all your sins and heals all your diseases. It is often preached that God forgives all our sins when we come to Him by faith, but what is often overlooked is the fact that He heals all our diseases too. The original Hebrew language that the Old Testament Bible (and the verse quoted from Psalm 103 above) was written in, translates the word all as "kol" which means each, every, totality, anything, everything and the whole of. He forgives all our sins and heals all our diseases. ALL. Whatever you have done or are suffering from is not too difficult for God to forgive or to heal.

Many people don't know what God's will is concerning healing. I've heard people say, "God is teaching me a lesson by giving me this disease" and "It's for His glory." That's just ridiculous! Jesus tells us that if even an imperfect earthly father who loves his children gives them good things, how much more will Father God give us good things when we ask for them (see Matthew 7:11).

Even if "He forgives all our sins and heals all our diseases" was the only verse in the whole Bible about healing and what God's will is, that would be enough. But it's always good to look at the whole of Scripture as well as just one verse, to understand God's character and will. So let's look at the Bible as a whole and see what the Word of God has to say about healing. I want you to be clear in your understanding that it is God's will to heal everyone, not just certain people or certain diseases, so that you can receive God's healing personally. God loves you so much.

For many years, churches have taught the gospel of salvation through Jesus. There has been much preaching and talk of salvation. This is essential because Jesus is the only way to God the Father, and Jesus is the only safe and legal access point into the spirit realm. However, salvation is not an end in itself but is the doorway into the whole kingdom of heaven, and that doorway is available for you to access the kingdom of heaven today. More than any other subject, Jesus taught on God's kingdom of heaven.

Jesus said, "I am the door. Whoever enters through me shall be saved and he can go in and out and find pasture" (John 10:9).

Jesus is the doorway into the kingdom of heaven and the legal access point into the realm of the spirit. The original Greek word for saved in this verse means saved from sin, healed physically, mentally and emotionally, delivered, set free and kept safe. So if you enter into the spirit realm through the Son of God (Jesus), then Jesus says you will be made whole and kept safe, but you must receive this through faith. He also says you can go in and out of the spirit realm and find pasture, which means peace, rest and sustenance for your soul.

Wouldn't you like that? Well, it's available to you through Jesus.

First of all, let's look at the subject of healing in the Old Testament, the first Covenant that was made between God and His people.

Healing under the Old Covenant

The Israelites were in slavery for 400 years in Egypt. Imagine the scene thousands of years ago: one million male slaves (plus women and children) being whipped, tortured and mistreated; forced against their will to build huge pyramids, living in the hot desert with their families in tents. Malnourished, in pain, with many illnesses and disabilities. Women giving birth with no anaesthetic nor medical help like we have today. There were probably around three million people in total; a whole nation of people miserable, sick and underfed. Then God raised up Moses and performed powerful signs and wonders through him in order for the people to be set free. The Bible says that miraculously the Israelites escaped from captivity and "He brought them out with silver and gold and none of them were feeble, weak, injured or stumbling." (Psalm 105:37). God healed them all. He said, "I am the Lord who heals you" (Exodus 15:26). And He did. God said that to about three million people. They all believed His word and every single one was healed and made whole.

Believe it or not, that's all under the Old Covenant and that is simply a shadow of what is available for us under the New Covenant through the blood of Jesus. It just gets better and better!

Remember the prophet I mentioned earlier named Isaiah? He prophesied around 750 years BC that Jesus would go to the cross to take away our sin and sickness and pain. This is what he prophesied:

"Who would have thought God's saving power would look like this?

The servant grew up before God—a scrawny
   seedling, a scrubby plant in a parched field.
There was nothing attractive about him,
   nothing to cause us to take a second look.
He was looked down on and passed over, a

man who suffered, who knew pain firsthand.
One look at him and people turned away. We
   looked down on him, thought he was scum.
But the fact is, it was our pains he carried—our
   disfigurements (our sickness, infirmities and
   disease), all the things wrong with us.
We thought he brought it on himself, that God
   was punishing him for his own failures.
But it was our sins that did that to him, that
   ripped and tore and crushed him—our sins!
He took the punishment, and that made us
   whole. Through his bruises (and wounds) we
   get healed.
We're all like sheep who've wandered off and
   gotten lost. We've all done our own thing,
   gone our own way.
And GOD has piled all our sins, everything
   we've done wrong, on him, on him.

He was beaten, he was tortured,
   but he didn't say a word.
Like a lamb taken to be slaughtered
   and like a sheep being sheared,
   he took it all in silence.
Justice miscarried, and he was led off -
   and did anyone really know what was
   happening?
He died without a thought for his own welfare,
   beaten bloody for the sins of my people.
They buried him with the wicked, threw him in
   a grave with a rich man,

Even though he'd never hurt a soul or said one
  word that wasn't true."
(Isaiah 53:1-9 The Message version of The Bible).

In verse 4 of this passage, the Hebrew word
'choliy' {khol-ee} which is translated as 'disfigurements'
here is often translated sickness, infirmities or disease
elsewhere, so I added it into the quote.

Fast forward more than 700 years when Jesus
walked on the earth, and His close friend and follower
Matthew wrote this about Him. In it, Matthew quotes
the passage above from Isaiah 53: "When evening
came, many who were full of evil spirits were brought
to him, and he drove out the spirits with a word and
healed all the sick. This was to fulfil what was spoken
through the prophet Isaiah 'He took up our infirmities
and carried our diseases'" (Matthew 8:16,17).

A fresh start

As we can clearly see in this prophecy from Isaiah,
Jesus the Messiah died in our place. He took up our
pain and our diseases. So if you are in pain or
tormented by the enemy, you can be set free. Imagine
right now that Jesus is standing in front of you. Why
not begin to thank Him for what He did for you? Speak
out loud if you can. Say, "Thank you Jesus that you
came to earth as a man. Thank you that even though
you didn't need to die, that you didn't need to do it, you
gave yourself for me. Thank you that you took all of my
pain, so I no longer need to have pain in my body."

Imagine yourself taking all that pain and torment and giving it to Jesus. Go on, you can actually lift it off yourself and give it to Him. He has taken it from you. You may already begin to feel the pain leaving your body as you say this out loud. You can also speak to the pain or the problem and command it to go. The only reason you have it is because the devil is a liar and has made you think that because you are human you are subject to sickness and decay. But actually you are not 'human' in the real meaning of the word if you have given your life to Jesus. You are a new creation; the old has gone and the new is here. You have a fresh start. (2 Corinthians 5:17). You are no longer confined to the pattern of this fallen world and to the lies of the enemy unless you come into agreement with them in your mind, your confession or your actions.

Thank Jesus for taking all your sins too!

"Praise the Lord oh my soul and don't forget He forgives all my sins and heals all my diseases" (Psalm 103:3-4).

You are never going to be the same again. I hope you're beginning to understand this now. Just think how your life is going to be different as you receive this divine healing. Start to visualize getting out of bed in the morning with no pain, no disability or illness. Full of life and energy and joy. That's what Jesus has done for you. It's for you; He did it for you. No matter how bad it's been or how bad you've been, you can be free, be forgiven and be made whole. You should be jumping around right now, thanking God for what He has done for you. He loves you so much. Let's release the anointing of the Holy Spirit right now for you; release the healing power of Jesus into your body and come into agreement with Heaven for your healing, your freedom and joy. Begin to praise God and thank Him for what He has done for you.

In the New Testament of the Bible, we discover that Father God made a new covenant with His people, through Jesus. John, one of Jesus' disciples and close friends, states that God loved you and me so much, that He sent His beloved son Jesus to die in our place (John 3:16). Because of the death and resurrection of Jesus Christ, the Son of God, we are able to live sinless and healthy lives.

If you haven't done so already, perhaps you'd like to ask Jesus to come into your life and make you brand new. You can have a fresh start now. Tell Him how you're feeling, maybe share with Him some of the things on your mind, any things you've done wrong, that made you feel shame, guilt or remorse. Any regrets? Share them with Him. Tell Him you're sorry. Ask Him to forgive you, to help you, to come into your life and set you free. He's been waiting for you to come to Him. He loves you.

You'll begin to feel lighter, more clear headed, peaceful and hopeful as you do this. Breathe in the Holy Spirit with a deep breath. Breath out all the lies, the hatred, the bitterness, anxiety, guilt and shame. Receive His love and His forgiveness. His joy is available for you. Relax. Be at peace. It's time to start really living life to the full.

Healing is for all

If you still haven't grasped the truth that healing through the power of Jesus is for everyone, including you, then read the following Scriptures:

One time, a man with leprosy came to Jesus and said, "If it be your will, make me clean." Jesus replied, "I will!" (Matthew 8:3). If you ask Him the same thing today, He will say to you, "I will."

"Great multitudes followed him, and he healed all their sick" (Matthew 12:15).

"All who touched him were healed" (Matthew 14:36).

"When the sun was setting, the people brought to Jesus all who had various kinds of sickness; and he laid his hands on every one of them and healed them" (Luke 4:40).

Acts 10:38 states "How God anointed Jesus of Nazareth with the Holy Spirit and with power and how He went about doing good and healing ALL that were oppressed by the enemy, for God was with Him."

The Bible states that Jesus Christ is the same yesterday, and today, and forever (see Hebrews 13:8). If He did it then, He will do it now, for you.

If we want to know what the will of God is, we can look at Jesus. He said, "Anyone who has seen me has seen the Father" (John 14:9).

Did Jesus put sickness on anyone? No. He healed those who came to Him and He loved to do it. Jesus came to break the power of the enemy; to destroy the devil's work (1 John 3:8). Sickness comes from the devil and Jesus has destroyed his work. He accomplished it all on the cross. Jesus declared, "It is finished!" (John 19:30).

CHAPTER FOUR

Demonstrations of Power

"For the message of the cross is foolishness to those who are perishing but to us who are being saved, it is the power of God." 1 Corinthians 1:18

Years ago I had a remarkable dream. It was long before I had any thoughts of preaching. I was a businesswoman at the time and had never preached, but in the dream I was preaching to a large group of people. The dream was very clear and I still remember it now, many years later. I was teaching about healing in the dream and telling people that the word in the original Greek translation of the Bible for healing is 'sozo.' I went on to explain that the words for deliverance and salvation in the New Testament are often from the original 'sozo' too. Then people in my dream began to be healed and delivered of evil spirits and many gave their lives to Jesus and received new life. When I awoke I thought it was strange as I had never heard the word 'sozo' before. But the dream seemed so real I decided to do some research and was shocked to discover that what I had been preaching in my dream was true. I love it when the Holy Spirit teaches us things in our dreams like that.

I went on to discover that the word is used many times in the Bible. The New Testament is translated into English from the original Greek it was written in and the word 'sozo' gets translated interchangeably. The same word 'sozo' can be translated healed, whole, saved, delivered, kept safe. For example, Romans 10:9: "If you confess with your mouth Jesus is Lord and believe in your heart that God raised Him from the dead, you will be saved (sozo)." Mark 6:56: "All who touched him were healed (sozo)." Mark 5:23: "My little daughter is dying. Please come and put your hands on her so that she will be healed (sozo) and live." Mark 16:16: "Whoever believes and is baptized shall be saved (sozo)." Luke 8:36: "...the demonized man had been cured (sozo)."

Saved and healed in our café

One day a guy came into our café in Blacon. He was the brother-in-law of our Kitchen Manager. He told us he had osteoporosis which meant his bones broke regularly. He explained that his little finger was strapped up because the bone had broken and he had just been to the hospital. He was in a lot of pain. We told him about Jesus, the fact that when He died on the cross, He took all of his sin, sickness and pain. The man said he wanted to pray to Jesus, so we sat at a table in the corner and he asked the Lord to forgive him for his sin and to heal him, because he understood that He had taken it all when He was crucified and rose from the dead. Instantly the man was forgiven and Jesus came into his life. He told me all the pain left his finger so I asked him if he could remove the bandage. He warned me that it would be nasty. He said his finger was completely broken and it would bend all the way back to touch the top of his hand. However, as he unwrapped the bandage, he was shocked to discover that not only had the pain gone, but his finger was unable to bend backwards and seemed to be perfectly normal. That's my Jesus!

"Don't forget all His benefits, He forgives all your sins and heals all your diseases. He redeems your life from the pit and crowns you with love and compassion. He satisfies your desires with good things so that your youth is renewed like the eagle's" (Psalm 103:3-5). How about receiving forgiveness and healing and having your youth restored? God is good and there are good things available to us when we follow Him with all our heart.

When Jesus went to the cross, He paid the price not only for all our sins but for all our diseases too. The Bible says, "...by His wounds we are healed." Sickness and disease were laid on Him when He was being flogged. "Everyone who calls on the name of the Lord will be saved" (Romans 10:13). The original meaning of that word saved is 'saved from eternal damnation, healed physically, mentally and emotionally, delivered from torment, made whole'.

Jesus is Lord. When we turn to Jesus, we can receive healing in every area of our lives.

Jesus said "These signs will accompany those who believe. In my name they will drive out demons... they will place their hands on sick people and they will get well" (Mark 16:17).

We are created in the image of God. God is spirit. When we turn to God through Jesus, we invite Jesus into our lives through His Holy Spirit. The Holy Spirit is God and He comes and lives in us. When Jesus lived on the earth He demonstrated love and power through the Holy Spirit. Jesus said that now He has gone back to be with the Father, we can do greater miracles than He did! (see John 14:12). We need the power of the Holy Spirit in our lives so that we can overcome sin and sickness and have exciting adventures with God. As followers of Jesus, we can bring the Kingdom of Heaven to the earth, wherever we go.

I love what the Apostle Paul said about the Kingdom of God, " So we fix our eyes not on what is seen, but on what is unseen, since what is seen is temporary, but what is unseen is eternal. (2 Corinthians 4:18).

The eternal is the unseen substance of what's in Heaven. In fact, the eternal, supernatural realm overrules the physical or natural realm. And that includes the physical symptoms of sickness, disease and pain that may be in your body, mind and emotions, as well as the physical circumstances in your life.

40

Jesus taught His followers to pray, "On earth as it is in heaven." As you agree with Jesus and invite the Kingdom of heaven to come through the Spirit of Jesus, He brings the realm of God, the Kingdom of Heaven to earth, from the spiritual into the physical realm.

The Kingdom of Heaven overrules the doctor's diagnosis and what you are feeling. It breaks the law of physics as we know it and the realm of the impossible. It begins to open up possibilities in your life and brings you hope. "The Kingdom of God has come upon you" (Matthew 12:28).

Jesus told a religious man called Nicodemus that no one could see or enter the Kingdom of God unless they are born again from above, born of the Spirit (see John 3:3,5).

The Apostle Paul declared that the good news of the Kingdom of God is the mighty miracle working power of God for salvation, freedom and healing for everyone who believes (see Romans 1:16).

I had a satanist contact me on FaceBook one time. She was desperate. She'd been given my book, 'A Diary of Miracles Part 1' to read by her leader, as apparently they wanted to study me and what I was up to. That book is packed full of miracle stories centered around the café we used to run in our 'deprived' neighborhood of Blacon, Chester. It is full of the miracle working power of Jesus.

As the satanist read my book, she was impacted by the Holy Spirit and the high level of power she encountered whilst reading it. Her friend John, also a satanist, was extremely tormented and sick in body, but she said her lord, satan, was unable to heal him even though she'd asked satan repeatedly. Of course, when she contacted me, I knew full well that satan is a liar and he comes to "kill, steal and destroy" but Jesus "comes to bring life in all its fullness" (see John 10:10). There really was no point in her trying to get satan to heal her friend. But as she read my book she received the revelation that Jesus is the highest power and that He has overcome satan and all the powers and principalities of darkness. The satanist was asking me if my Lord, Jesus, could heal her friend's broken fingers and set him free from torment. He would scream through the night every time he slept and his fingers were repeatedly broken.

Firstly, the Holy Spirit told me her real name, despite the fact that she was using a satanic name. Then I told her that of course Jesus could and would heal her friend. I asked Jesus to walk into his bedroom that night, that John would put his broken fingers into the wounds in Jesus' hands where He was nailed to the cross and that he would be healed and set free from torment.

The next day the satanist messaged me saying she couldn't believe it, but Jesus had healed her friend John's hands; they were no longer broken, and the tormenting demons had left, enabling him to sleep soundly. I tell you, there is wonder-working supernatural power in the name and the blood of Jesus.

"The Kingdom of God is not just a matter of talk but of power" (1 Corinthians 4:20).

The Apostle Paul said, "For our gospel did not come to you in word only, but also in power...." (1 Thessalonians 1:5).

"And my speech and my preaching were not with persuasive words of human wisdom, but in demonstration of the Spirit and of power."(1 Corinthians 2:4).

God made a covenant with you, through the blood of Jesus when He was flogged, died on the cross and rose from the grave. By His blood we are forgiven of sins and by His wounds, healed of sickness (see Matthew 26:28, 1 Peter 2:24).

It's time for you to experience and encounter the power of God in your life. You're hearing powerful stories and reading words of truth in this book, but you also need to encounter the divine power available to you through Jesus. Receive it now. It's available to you. I release the power of the Spirit of Jesus for you. By faith, apply it to your mind, your body, your emotions or whatever area of your life is in need. God loves you. He is for you. He wants you well.

At a recent workshop in Texas, I saw a guy coming through the door as I was meeting the attendees. Timothy had come as he wanted to learn how to heal the sick, but he also needed a miracle himself. The first thing I noticed was that he was shaking uncontrollably.

He had severe tremors. He also walked slowly; with each step, he had to look at the floor to see where to put his foot. He explained that 33 years previously, when in the Military, he had been electrocuted in a bad accident. He had woken up in hospital and the doctors were surprized that he had survived. But as a result, he had lost all feeling in his body, apart from the thumb and forefinger of his right hand. He also had severe tremors throughout his body.

During the session on healing, I taught some Scriptural truths and shared miracle stories that I'd witnessed. Then, as is usually my custom, I ask people to pair up and have a go at releasing the healing power of Jesus. A young guy partnered with Timothy and they prayed with each other. A few moments later I could hear shouts of joy coming from them. I invited Timothy up to the front of the workshop and he shared with everyone what had just taken place. All feeling had miraculously returned to his body and the tremors had reduced dramatically, he reckoned by 85%. I noticed a marked difference in him.

That afternoon he removed his shoes and socks and walked barefoot on the grass outside, enjoying being able to feel for the first time in 33 years. He marvelled at the heat on the door handle from the hot sun and didn't care that it was burning his hand, he was so happy to be able to feel again. The following day he shared with everyone how the tremors had completely ceased overnight (we have video footage showing the dramatic healing). He showed us evidence of his handwriting when he took notes in the first session which looked like a young child's writing, compared with the notes he took later that day after he was healed, which were perfectly neat because his hands were no longer shaking.

The day after the workshop, Timothy visited a neighbor to show him what God had done for him. His neighbor needed two new knees, so Timothy released the power of Jesus and immediately his neighbor's knees were healed. Now he doesn't require surgery and is free from pain.

God is good and what He did for Timothy and his neighbor, he wants to do for you too!

CHAPTER FIVE

Free Yourself

*"Forgiveness is unlocking the door to set someone free
and realizing you were the prisoner"*
- Max Lucado

One day a woman came into our café to meet a friend for coffee. I found out she hardly knew anything about Jesus as I began to describe some of the miracles we'd witnessed in there. She showed me her knees. They were both swollen like melons and apparently very painful. She had been diagnosed with infected arthritis and had difficulty walking. I began to tell her how Jesus died on the cross for her and how he had taken all sickness and all sin, when I had the feeling she perhaps needed to forgive someone.

I asked her if that was the case. She looked down and nodded. She told me she couldn't forgive her husband for something he'd done, but felt it was eating away at her. So I led her in a prayer where she said, "I choose to forgive my husband for what he has done and I ask you Father God to forgive me for all my sin. Jesus, I ask you to come into my life and I receive your forgiveness and your healing by faith. Thank you that you died in my place and you rose again. Come and fill me with your Holy Spirit."

She prayed that out loud and sitting right there in our café I watched as the grey pained expression in her face ebbed away. The colour returned to her cheeks, she began to breathe more slowly, her eyes brightened and she smiled. We all looked down and watched her huge knees literally shrink before our eyes. Within a matter of seconds they were back to their normal size. She swung her legs backwards and forwards, stood up quickly and was walking and jumping and thanking God for all that He had done.

Over the years I've come to realize that one of the main blockages to people receiving their healing and freedom is that they have withheld forgiveness from someone who has hurt or offended them. Forgiveness is a huge issue and, believe it or not, unforgiveness is the root cause of many diseases, maladies, mental illnesses, emotional problems and lack of joy. These include arthritis and other joint problems, cancer, depression, anger, bitterness, headaches, back and shoulder problems, digestive issues and many more besides. That's not to say that all of these conditions are always caused by lack of forgiveness but they can be.

When God came to earth as the man Jesus, He willingly laid down His life for you and me and He even chose to forgive those who tortured and murdered Him. Because of His death and resurrection,

He made it possible for God the Father to forgive all our sin. However, Jesus Himself shared a story making it clear that if we want to receive forgiveness by God and live in freedom, then we need to forgive others. It doesn't get much clearer than this:

"Then Peter came to Jesus and asked, "Lord, how many times shall I forgive my brother or sister who sins against me? Up to seven times?" Jesus answered, "I tell you, not seven times, but seventy times seven. "Therefore, the kingdom of heaven is like a king who wanted to settle accounts with his servants. As he began the settlement, a man who owed him ten thousand bags of gold was brought to him. Since he was not able to pay, the master ordered that he and his wife and his children and all that he had be sold to repay the debt. At this the servant fell on his knees before him. 'Be patient with me,' he begged, 'and I will pay back everything.' The servant's master took pity on him, cancelled the debt and let him go.

But when that servant went out, he found one of his fellow servants who owed him a hundred silver coins. He grabbed him and began to choke him. 'Pay back what you owe me!' he demanded. His fellow servant fell to his knees and begged him, 'Be patient with me, and I will pay it back.' But he refused. Instead, he went off and had the man thrown into prison until he could pay the debt. When the other servants saw what had happened, they were outraged and went and told their master everything that had happened. Then the master called the servant in. 'You wicked servant,' he said, 'I cancelled all that debt of yours because you begged me to. Shouldn't you have had mercy on your fellow servant just as I had on you?'

In anger his master handed him over to the jailers to be tortured, until he should pay back all he owed. This is how my heavenly Father will treat each of you unless you forgive your brother or sister from your heart" (Matthew 18:21-35).

When you don't forgive someone, you become imprisoned. It isn't God or even the other person keeping you in jail; it's you. The original Greek word used here for 'jailers' also means 'tormentors' and 'torturers'. Disease or pain can be like torture and make you feel tormented. If you feel that way, it may simply be that you need to forgive someone.

It's important to realize that forgiving someone does not mean that what they did to you was okay. You may have suffered terrible atrocities, cruelties, physical or verbal abuse, abandonment, rejection, pain and resulting fear, breakdown and disfunction. What they did may have altered the course of your life dramatically and caused you to make unwise or difficult choices. You may now be very bitter or resentful. However, it is extremely important that you choose to forgive that person. As I quoted at the beginning of this chapter, 'Forgiveness is unlocking the door to set someone free and realizing the prisoner was you'. The decision that you are about to make has the power to transform your life. Seriously. So let's take some time to do this now.

Practical activation

Begin by telling God you are sorry for holding grudges, seeking revenge, wanting bad things to happen and not forgiving others. Then ask this: "Holy Spirit, please show me who I need to forgive."

You may find it helpful to grab a pen and paper or use your phone or computer and write a list of all the people the Holy Spirit shows you. Usually the first person, or people, to pop into your thoughts are those you need to forgive. If you think about that person and you want to hurt them or you feel fear, rejection, anger or some other negative thought, then chances are, you need to forgive them. Harboring those feelings towards them will only cause you problems; mental, emotional, spiritual and/or physical.

Why not start at the top of the list and write this sentence out for each person you need to forgive: "I choose to forgive (so and so) for when they (speak out what they did to you) and for making me feel (write down how you felt as a result, such as anger, fear, rejection, abandonment). Write out that sentence for every person who has just popped into your mind.

Next, read the sentences out loud, one at a time. You may need to read each sentence more than once until you really mean it. And do speak out loud if you can, even if it's just a whisper, as words are very powerful in the spirit realm. As you begin to speak the words out, you will find that those feelings of anger, fear and so on will begin to lift.

Then I suggest that you tell any evil spirit that has attached itself to you through those negative emotions to leave. You can say something like this:

"Father God, forgive me for coming into agreement with fear (or anger or whatever emotion you've been feeling in connection with what happened). I command every spirit of fear (or anger etc) to leave me now in the name of Jesus." Once you have said that out loud, you could take a deep breath in of the Holy Spirit and breathe or cough out the evil spirits, one at a time until they have all left. You may sense darkness or heaviness leaving and feel much lighter and brighter. If you need help with this, then seek out a trusted Christian friend. I explain more about getting rid of evil spirits in another chapter and also in my book 'How to be Free from Demons'.

Once you have done all that, you can go back to your list and write 'I FORGIVE YOU' next to each person's name. Then start to pray for the person you've just forgiven. Pray that they will know Jesus, that they will be free and healed and know God's love. It's powerful when you do this.

You may find that you can do all this fairly quickly and easily, or it may take you a few days to really come to the decision to truly forgive. But once you have done this, a fresh start awaits you. I'd love to hear from you and find out how your life has changed once you've forgiven those who've hurt you. Do write me a message and let me know; my details are at the back of this book.

Make a conscious decision that from now on, every time someone hurts you (whether on purpose or without knowing), choose to forgive them straight away. It will help you to stay sane, happy, healthy and younger looking too!

You may find that as you do this exercise, your body begins to feel better straight away. Aches and pains may subside, digestive problems ease and tension leaves. You may also find you are sleeping better. Feel free to tell those problems to leave you, through the power of Jesus and start living the first day of the rest of your life with a brand new outlook. Here's to a new you!

CHAPTER SIX

Healing Angels, Portals and Anointings

Some time ago, I was chatting to a woman and saw a huge bright flash just behind her shoulder as we were talking. Often when I see a flash I know it's an angel, but I like to know what the angel is doing or why I am seeing it. So as with most things, I ask the Holy Spirit what I have just seen. As I did this, the first thought in my mind was 'Healing Angel'. Rather than just ignore it and carry on, I began to question why a healing angel may be standing right behind this young woman. So I interrupted our conversation by saying something like, "I've just seen a bright flash behind your shoulder and I think it may be a healing angel. Do you happen to have a problem with your shoulder or something around this area?" She replied that she'd had a long term problem with that shoulder. She'd had physio and was on medication and said she may require surgery as it was causing her a lot of pain and wasn't improving.

I thought this would be a great opportunity to release healing for her shoulder. I thanked God for sending His angels, I placed my hand on her shoulder and said, "I release the power of Jesus to heal your shoulder." She felt something move in that area, the pain lifted and she was able to lift her arm freely; something she couldn't do before. She realized she was completely healed. We thanked God for what He had done, and I was encouraged to search out the Scriptures for more references to angels.

Angels are commonplace in the Bible. They are messengers from God sent to earth from heaven, helping to put His plans into action and bringing messages from God to people. They are "Ministering spirits sent by God to serve those who will inherit salvation" and are "Mighty ones who do His word" (see Hebrews 1:14 and Psalm 103:20).

Sometimes when we see an angel and recognize them as such, it's easy to be full of awe and even worship them, but Scripture makes it clear not to worship angels; they are 'fellow servants', serving God alongside us (see Revelation 19:10).

In addition, the Bible is clear that we should not pray to angels, or to anyone else for that matter, apart from God: Jesus is the only mediator between us and God (see 1 Timothy 2:5). But the Bible is full of people encountering angels and heavenly messengers and talking to them. Often they will bring us a message from God.

When I started to honor the angels for what they do, and invited them to come from the spirit realm and manifest in the physical, natural realm, I began to be aware of angels much more than I had been up until that point. You could try doing this too.

Angels are sent on assignments by God and we are often unaware of them, but sometimes we see them or become more aware of them like I did with the woman I just mentioned. In the time when Jesus was on the earth, there was a certain pool named 'Bethesda' in Jerusalem. From time to time, an angel would come and stir up the water in the pool. The first to enter the water after it was stirred were healed (see John 5:4). Because of this, it was a gathering place for many people with disabilities and diseases, all hoping to get into the water and receive healing.

John records that Jesus came to the pool during a festival He was attending, and He spoke to one of the disabled men lying near the pool. Jesus discovered that the man had been disabled for thirty eight years and asked him, "Do you want to get well?" The man probably wondered at such a strange question, since he was lying near the pool of healing and he was obviously disabled. But he didn't give a straight answer. Instead, he gave reasons why he had not been healed: he had no-one to carry him into the water when it was stirred by the angel, which meant someone else always beat him to it.

Jesus didn't get into a discussion with him, but He simply said, "Get up! Pick up your mat and walk" (John 5:8). The man was instantly cured.

This man was unable to walk or even crawl into the water and so he remained paralyzed. But Jesus saw Him. Jesus sees you too. No matter how long you've put up with the sickness or the disease or the pain. Whether you were born with disabilities, whether your problems are the result of an accident, injury, surgery, condition, generational, medication or even self-inflicted, God knows what you are going through. He wants to heal you.

Do you want to be well? If the answer is YES, you can be well. Why wait any longer? He loves you. Simply believe and receive all the good things He has for you. What a wonderful Savior He is. There's no need to go into detail or give explanations about your problems. Jesus already knows and He has already paid the price for your infirmities, so you may as well simply receive your healing right away.

This passage shows it's okay to receive healing from angels, but the key thing is that when angels visit, they will always lead you to Jesus and they will glorify Him. In this passage, even though there was a healing angel around, it was the power of Jesus who made the man well and it's still the same for us today. Evil spirits can sometimes trick us by appearing as angels of light (see 2 Corinthians 11:14) but an evil spirit will not glorify Jesus or want you to know Jesus better. An evil spirit will not release the Father's love for you like the Holy Spirit does. If healing comes from an evil spirit, it will be temporary, counterfeit and will probably cost you money and in the long run most likely your health or something worse.

Healing portals

Often in history, fountains, spas and pools of water are attributed to having healing properties. Water can be soothing and beneficial when it contains certain minerals and salts and people have reported health benefits from visiting some of these places and 'taking the waters'. One of these is in Holywell (pronounced Hollywell) in North Wales, close to our home city of Chester. Over the years, many have visited this place for healing. One day whilst some friends from Germany were staying with us, we had the idea to go to St Winifred's Well in Holywell. I'd never been before, but we thought it would be a good opportunity to visit and see what it was all about.

God can use anything for His purposes. While we were there and looking around, we noticed a woman ahead of us who was obviously visiting the pool for some healing. She had canes that were helping her to walk but she looked to be in pain and walked with difficulty.

We approached her and got chatting. She told me she was diagnosed with a serious disease at the age of twenty one, she'd also had recent surgery for a triple heart bypass, she had narrowing of the arteries and blood clots and had been told her case was terminal. On top of all this, she'd had an MRI scan on her knee which was completely shattered and all the cartilage had gone. She needed a new knee but was unable to have surgery due to her heart condition and the surgeon told her she would die on the operating table if they were to attempt the operation. Almost all hope had gone, but she'd come to the healing well as she didn't know what else to do.

We began to tell her about Jesus and that He could heal all her diseases. She seemed keen to give it a go, so we prayed with her and released the power of Jesus into her body. All the pain instantly disappeared from her knee and she told us she could feel a warm glow covering her body. We have a video showing her walking freely with no pain, no stiffness and no sticks!

Sometimes there are places and portals where the power of God seems to be more tangible than others and it may be where a significant event occurred. There can be a healing presence, or anointing residing there.

In 2 Kings 13:21, we read about the prophet Elisha. When he died, his bones were buried in a cave. "Once while some Israelites were burying a man, suddenly they saw a band of raiders; so they threw the man's body into Elisha's tomb. When the body touched Elisha's bones, the man came to life and stood up on his feet."

While he was alive, Elisha performed many miracles through the power of the Holy Spirit. The anointing that was on his life was so powerful that it remained in his bones after he had died. And that was under the Old Covenant. Think how much more the power of Jesus can accomplish now we are under the New Covenant!

The book of Acts in the New Testament is packed full of incredible miracles and supernatural experiences, recording just some of what went on with Jesus' followers after Jesus had ascended to heaven. In chapter five of the book of Acts, we read how these followers were performing such amazing signs and wonders that crowds of sick and tormented people were brought to the streets, many lying on mats and beds so that at least Peter's shadow would pass over them and heal them (see Acts 5:15). This sounds extraordinary but is available to us too. It's because Peter was "clothed with power from on high" (Luke 24:49); the Holy Spirit of Jesus. We too can receive His power in this way when we follow Jesus.

The Apostle Paul understood this. We read how, "God did extraordinary miracles through Paul, so that even handkerchiefs and aprons that had touched him were taken to the sick, and their illnesses were cured and the evil spirits left them" (Acts 19:11-12). It may seem strange, but the powerful anointing of the Holy Spirit can be transferred from one to another, even through bones and cloth - in fact any way that God so chooses. That's why simply through picking up this book you may have experienced a miracle of healing or deliverance from evil spirits, even before you began to read it.

This book contains powerful words from God; it is full of truths from His Word, the Bible. As I'm writing this, I'm asking the Lord to pour out His Holy Spirit upon you as you hold this book and as you read it, even if you're reading an electronic version! God is all powerful. He knows what you need and He is willing and able to do it for you now.

Let's pray together and thank God for His angels and His healing anointing:

"Father God, thank you for your angels. I honor them and all that they do in obedience to you Lord. Thank you that your angels protect me, that they guard my ways, they lift me up, they communicate messages from you and they bring blessings such as healing. Help me to be more aware of your angels. I invite messengers from heaven, sent by God to come and help me, to bring healing and wholeness, to minister to me in accordance with God's good plans for my life. I want to receive everything you have for me, Lord.

Please open my eyes and all my senses to see your angelic messengers. Help me believe that your Word is true, that what happened in the Bible can happen to me today. Thank you for your tangible healing anointing, that it is available for me right now through the pages of this book and from your presence, Jesus. I receive your healing power now as I open up my life to you and your ways, Jesus."

Now look around and be aware of any lights, flashes, shimmers, unusual breezes or tingling in your body, a warm feeling or a sense that someone is touching you. It may well be an angel. Simply receive.

CHAPTER SEVEN

Blockages to Healing

You can receive healing right now in your spirit, soul and body; in fact you may have been healed already through reading the previous chapters or simply from picking up this book. God has done everything to make healing available to you and He wants you well even more than you do! However, if you have been asking for healing and not yet received it, or praying for others and nothing seems to have happened, then this chapter is for you.

I've covered below some blockages to healing that I have come across when praying for others. Read through them with an open heart and ask the Holy Spirit to show you what may be preventing you receiving the healing that is available to you through Jesus.

"Father God, I ask you to show me anything that is getting in the way of me receiving the healing that was made possible for me when Jesus went to the cross. Holy Spirit, please make it clear to me. I tell every evil spirit to be quiet in the name of Jesus. Lord God I give you all my hopes, my desires, my disappointments, pride, unbelief and anything else that may get in the way of me receiving healing from you today. Amen."

I have listed below some potential blockages that may have prevented you from receiving your healing in the past. Read them with an open, humble heart.

Unbelief

Hopefully if you've read this far, you won't have any unbelief left! Some people may not believe that God's will is to heal them and they may not believe in Jesus, but they can still be healed. Read this excerpt from my book, "A Diary of Miracles Part 2":

"Monday 5 April

It's a Bank holiday, so the staff and volunteers got a day off, but we wanted the shop to be open so Rob and I worked in there today. A musician from Liverpool came in and was telling us that a musical he'd written the score for is being aired this weekend on the radio. He was limping so I asked him what the trouble was. He told me he'd suffered from sciatica for years. The sciatic nerve in his leg was trapped and it caused him a lot of pain but the doctors were unable to remedy it. I told him about the power of Jesus. He explained that he was an atheist and didn't believe in God at all, but I told him that God believed in him all the same and convinced him to let me have a go at praying for him. I told him, "If there isn't a God, nothing will happen. But if there is a God, then give Him chance to prove Himself."

I was surprised that he let me pray for him, but I released healing through Jesus and asked him, "Were you in pain before I prayed?" He told me that he was in a lot of pain. I said, "What is the pain like now?" and he replied that he could feel no pain, even when he bent over and did squats. He said that was unusual and he looked very surprised. His wife, who was standing behind him, said, "See! I told you there was a God." He was speechless."

So, you don't even need to believe in Jesus to be healed. However, I would say that if you want to stay healed and live in good health, then you need to follow Jesus. I talk more about this in the chapter on staying healed.

Jesus made it clear that even just a tiny bit of faith is all it takes. When someone lets me pray for them, whether they're an atheist or not, I believe that they are exerting a small amount of faith by letting me pray.

Jesus said, "Truly I tell you, if you have faith as small as a mustard seed, you can say to this mountain, 'Move from here to there,' and it will move. Nothing will be impossible for you." (Matthew 17:20). A mustard seed is tiny, so never worry about not having enough faith. Just step out and give it a go and see what happens.

Unbelief is different from lack of faith. Real unbelief can be an evil spirit. If you want to believe but find there is something always stopping you, or preventing you from believing, then treat it like an evil spirit. Ask God to forgive you for coming into agreement with that thing whether it's through words you've spoken or things you've done in the past that were full of unbelief, and tell that evil spirit to leave you in the name of Jesus.

There was a boy who was unable to speak and he suffered dangerous seizures. You can imagine how desperate the boy's parents were. Perhaps, like this boy, there is someone in your family who needs a miracle. One day, this boy's father met Jesus when He was on the earth. The man said to Jesus, "If you can do anything, take pity on us and help us." "'If you can'?" said Jesus. "Everything is possible for one who believes." Immediately the boy's father exclaimed, "I do believe; help me overcome my unbelief!" (Mark 9:22-24). Jesus healed the boy immediately.

Perhaps like this man, you too can say, "Jesus, help me overcome my unbelief." Just wanting to be free from unbelief is all the faith you need for a miracle. However, if it's a spirit of unbelief and you don't tell it to go, it can form a blockage. The spirit of unbelief, which is an evil spirit, can prevent you from receiving your healing. You may be surprized to hear that even Jesus Himself was unable to do many miracles in some places. His friend Matthew reports that when Jesus was teaching in his home town, the people became offended by Him and Jesus could not do many miracles "because of their unbelief" (Matthew 13:58). If even Jesus Himself was unable to do miracles because of unbelief, then if you are harboring a spirit of unbelief, it is unlikely you will be able to receive healing until you get rid of it.

Lack of worth

I've met people who are unable to receive healing because they feel unworthy of receiving healing from Jesus. Well, I have to tell you that's actually false humility, even pride. Jesus died for you. It cost Him everything. None of us are worthy but He has made us worthy, even if your illness or pain is as a result of your own foolishness or wrong choices. He has bought us with a price, so why not thank Him for what He has done for you and gladly receive everything He has made available to you by His torture, horrific death and glorious resurrection? Ask Him to forgive you for false humility or for not wanting to receive what He has done for you and just receive it. It will change your life.

Believing satan's lies

Satan is the father of lies and often what we assume are our own thoughts are in fact lies from the pit of hell. I've had some people tell me, "God doesn't want me healed yet as it's bringing Him glory." That statement is one of those thoughts from hell. That God can be glorified by making you sick is anathema to me. Satan will keep you from knowing the truth as long as he can, but thankfully you have now heard the truth and you can be set free. Simply ask God to forgive you for believing that lie, tell the lying spirit to leave you and be healed. It's as easy as that!

Soon after I met Beth, she told me she'd had back surgery years ago and showed me the huge scars on her back from the surgery. She'd been left with nerve pain ever since and it was often severe enough to make her cry, cause her to limp and have to give up many of the things she loved to do. This had been going on for years. She was unable to get up from her chair as she was telling me about the pain. Pain medication didn't seem to offer her any relief at all.

I told her, "It's a lie of the enemy. There is nothing wrong with you. It's simply a lying, deceiving spirit causing all this pain." She looked shocked, but began to believe me. I said, "Come on, jump up on your feet and walk". She said, "Oh I can't get up it hurts too much." But as she was saying that and I was encouraging her, she started to believe the truth that there really was nothing wrong with her. She jumped up from her chair and began to walk. I walked with her, she asked God to forgive her for believing the lying spirit and for coming into agreement with the spirit of pain and she told them to leave her at the name of Jesus. She continued walking, getting faster and faster, and the demons left one by one. The pain completely went and she was set free by Jesus there and then. Knowing that it was just a lying spirit has changed her life. It could change yours too.

Sometimes you have to fight

Generally when I pray for someone they get healed straight away. But it could be that you have been prayed for many times by many people and you're wondering if it will ever happen for you. It could be that you simply need the revelation of what Jesus has done for you. You may need to ask God to forgive you for coming into agreement with disappointment or disillusionment and then you can receive your healing.

I would always recommend that we treat illness, pain and sickness as a vicious animal. Sometimes when I'm asking the Holy Spirit how to pray for someone I'll have a dream or a vision of a ferocious animal; it could be a dog, a snake or lion and sometimes I've dreamed of a hybrid animal that's a cross between two species. The Holy Spirit will show me how to pray in each case but it seems to help you fight it yourself when you know it's attacking you. Do not give it any concessions. As the saying goes, 'Give it an inch and it will take a mile!'

I'll give you a couple of examples from my own life. Some years ago I was in severe pain with kidney stones. They seemed to come out of the blue and it was right before a trip to America where I was going to be speaking at a number of places in various States. The last thing I wanted was kidney stones. People are right when they say the pain is similar to childbirth; well the early stages of labour at least! I remember having a business meeting and I had to conduct the whole meeting lying down, the pain was so bad. But I didn't want to have any surgery or treatment, so I decided I was going to contend for my own healing.

I spoke to the kidney stones and said something like, "I command the pain to leave me now in the name of Jesus and don't come back." The pain left. I then decided, rather than tell the stones to disappear, that I wanted to see them so I knew they'd left. So I said, "Kidney stones, I command you to come out of my body but cause no pain." I had no pain and was able to fly without any problems, but I still hadn't seen the stones leave my body. I remember being in the States and an old gospel song came into my head: "The angel rolled the stone away." I began to sing, "The angel rolls the stones away" and made everyone laugh. Without getting into too much detail, over the next couple of days, I could feel a slight tickle, as though someone lightly had their finger on my back, it moved around my side and the next thing I knew, I went to the bathroom and, lo and behold, a pile of stones. Pretty big ones actually but no pain whatsoever. I was relieved in more ways than one! God is so good. But I had to do my bit: I chose not to have treatment, did not come into agreement with it, I spoke to the problem and told it what to do, I stepped out in faith, trusted God and received my healing.

I rarely get ill nowadays, but over the years I've had similar outcomes when something potentially problematic has had to leave my body. One time I felt a lump in my breast. I already knew it was the enemy but it became clear to me later that day when a letter from the hospital dropped through the letterbox inviting me for a mammogram, saying that even though mammograms are not usually offered to the under fifties, they'd decided to offer me one all the same and that I'd been selected randomly. I had to laugh. The enemy had really overplayed his hand there. Needless to say, I threw the letter away, didn't tell anyone about the lump as I didn't want to speak out negative words or come into agreement with that lie in any way, and I told the lump to disappear. It took a couple of months but one time as I put my finger on it and told it to go, it instantly disappeared and hasn't returned. That was a number of years ago now.

Disobedience to God can block your healing.

Many years ago there was a guy named Naaman who was Commander of King Aram's army in what is now Syria. He was a brave warrior but had a terrible skin disease known as leprosy. He heard that God could heal him, so he went in search of Elisha, a prophet who could help him. But when he arrived at Elisha's house, he became offended because Elisha didn't come and see him in person. Instead, he sent a messenger to instruct Naaman to go and bathe in the river seven times in order for him to be cured.

Naaman was angered so much by this, he wouldn't do it. He wanted Elisha to pray with him and 'wave his hand' so that he could be cured (see 2 Kings 5). Very often, disobedience to God is stubborn pride. I think I've offended a few people who have expected me to 'wave my hand' over them and heal them, but instead I ask someone else nearby to pray for them. This ensures everyone knows the healing is not from me but from Jesus and also enables the other person praying to experience a miracle too, often for the first time.

Jesus invites us all to follow Him, lay down our lives and go heal the sick, drive out demons, raise people from the dead and share the good news of the Kingdom of God. However, many people prefer a certain person to pray for them or want to be healed in a particular way and won't allow God to heal them His way. It's important to be obedient to the Holy Spirit.

Thankfully in this story, Naaman relented; he obediently dipped himself in the River Jordan seven times, his disfigured flesh was restored and his skin became like that of a young boy's. It wasn't the Jordan that healed Naaman, it was obedience to God. And it's interesting to note that Elisha would not take any form of payment from Naaman.

Disappointment and discouragement.

You may have been sick for a long time and tried all sorts of remedies to no avail. But it's very important not to give up. Do not give in to the sickness. It is not from God. Sickness is from the devil.

In this day and age it's easy to take medication or get some kind of 'quick fix' to ease the symptoms, but usually those things simply cause other problems and side effects and they don't actually deal with the root cause of the problem. But God can do that.

The enemy wants you to simply give in to the symptoms and live a second rate life. Jesus said that Satan comes to steal, kill and destroy, and you can see the way he has tried to do that in your life and your family's lives. But Jesus comes to bring life and a long, full, healthy life is available through the power of Jesus (see John 10:10). However, you have a choice. You have to make the decision not to allow satan's plan to be fulfilled in your life, but to choose the good plan that God has for you.

Don't allow disappointment, disillusionment, tiredness, pride, hopelessness, 'poor me' syndrome, jealousy of others or any other thing to rob you of a good, full life that Jesus has made possible for you.

At a conference some years ago I was speaking at an afternoon breakout session on healing. It was a fairly small group of around forty people. Just before I started to speak, a woman in the group raised her hand and said, "I just want to let you know that I'm right off healing. Me and my friends were full of faith and prayed for my friend's teenage son to be healed of a serious illness but he died. We've been so discouraged since then, that we're off healing altogether." I thought sarcastically, "Great! That's really going to encourage the group before I even start", but I said, "OK, well let's see what happens" and I took it as a challenge and an opportunity for God to break through.

As part of the session I got people to have a go at praying for each other for healing after I shared 'words of knowledge' to identify those who needed healing. One woman came forward with a seemingly impossible problem: she had broken her back ten years earlier. This had resulted in surgery that involved fusing vertebrae together and inserting metal pins and rods. She was still in severe pain ten years later despite morphine medication and was unable to bend to pick up her child. I wondered who I should choose to have a go at praying for her, and I thought, "I know, I'll choose the disappointed woman who's 'right off healing'!" So I asked her to come forward and pray for the woman with the broken back. Thankfully, she was willing to give it a go and as she did, the woman with the broken back began to scream with joy as the broken bones went back into place, the pain and the feeling of heavy weight she'd had for ten years lifted right off her and she was jumping around, crying with joy and hugging her friends. You can watch this video and others mentioned in this book on the playlist 'How to be healed' on my website www.alisscresswell.com.

The woman who, at the start of the session had told everyone she was 'off healing', was now saying, "That has so boosted me. When I prayed I was tingling from head to foot."

I personally prayed for people for healing and I didn't see any results for twelve years! Either people seemed to get worse, or I'd catch what they had and some even died. It was awful, and I was tempted to give up. Family and friends were telling me that it wasn't helping people and could be raising up their hopes just to have them dashed, and that perhaps it would be kinder to everyone if I just gave up. But I read the Bible and I believed what I read. I read books about other people following Jesus and seeing miracles when they prayed for others. I chose to persevere, to keep going when everything looked impossible. And then it happened. An amazing miracle, and the miracles haven't stopped ever since. I discovered that I wasn't just contending all those years for my own breakthrough, but for other people's too. So don't give up, whether you're needing healing in your own body or want to see others get well. It will happen and it could be today!

Why not ask God to forgive you for causing a blockage to receiving His healing in any way? Let's do that now:

"Father God, please forgive me for coming into agreement with the enemy's lies. Please show me right now Holy Spirit if I've caused your healing to be blocked in my life."

Now if something pops into your head, it could well be the Holy Spirit showing you. Go right ahead and ask God to forgive you for that thing and ask Him to help you and to heal you now.

CHAPTER EIGHT

Could it be a Demon?

I have already covered a number of reasons why you may not have received healing in the past, but I chose to take a whole chapter on this one. In fact, my next book is all about evil spirits; how to recognize and deal with them, but since a lot of illness is caused directly by evil spirits I wanted to cover this here. Many of you reading this book will be healed when you discover the truth that your sickness may simply be caused by an evil spirit. At the end of this chapter I'll lead you in a prayer that can get rid of these things once and for all and could very well change your life forever.

One day a woman and her husband came into the shop we ran named 'Spirit', in Chester UK. She had seen the blackboard propped up against a chair outside which read, 'Free Healings & Miracles' and had stepped inside the shop, intrigued. You see, Angela had been suffering from debilitating pain and tiredness for many years. Her husband Colin was no longer able to work, as his full-time job entailed caring for Angela.

I was standing behind the counter when she approached me. "Excuse me", she said in a shaky voice. "I notice on your sign that you are offering free miracles and I really need one." This request was a daily occurrence in our shop and so I began to chat to her. I asked what the problem was. Many people tell me their maladies in detail as though I'm a doctor looking to diagnose the problem, but I am no medic and don't really need to know all the details because Jesus knows and His power is the perfect remedy for every ailment known to man.

Angela explained that she had ME, some sort of chronic fatigue, as well as fibromyalgia – severe pain throughout her body. The two walking canes with which she propped herself up gave testimony to the fact it was difficult for her to walk. She told me she had also suffered terrible problems with her abdomen and had undergone surgery but it still wasn't right. She had recurring migraine headaches and painful arthritis. My heart went out to her as it was obvious she'd had enough of all these pains and physical problems. Unfortunately, the doctors could do nothing else but prescribe her pain relief which had little effect. Her husband sat down and ordered a coffee but his face showed no sign of rest; he'd obviously had enough too.

Angela begged me, "Please, is there anything you can do to help me?" As she was speaking, I was listening to my friend Holy Spirit and also thinking of similar situations I'd witnessed before. A thought popped into my head, so I asked Angela if she had ever been involved with 'reiki' healing. She looked surprized, but said that yes, she was a 'Reiki Master'. I asked her exactly when the trouble started, and she looked shocked as the realization set in. She replied, "About the same time I started learning reiki."

I went on to explain that the few people I had met who were involved with reiki seemed to be ill, tired, depressed or unhappy in some way. I told her that I believed the symptoms and conditions she'd described to me were caused by evil spirits. I said that was no problem for the power of Jesus, as He had defeated satan and every evil spirit when He laid down His life for us and was crucified. That He had offered up his back to be lashed and that every sickness and pain had been placed on Him. That on the cross He paid the price for our sin. That He had been raised from the dead and in so doing, He had not only been given power over sin and sickness and pain, but also over death.

I went on to explain that it was easy for her to be healed and set free; all she needed to do was receive the healing and forgiveness from God through Jesus Christ. I did give her one word of warning though: I said that Jesus described how evil spirits could be sent out of a person but sometimes they may go and find more evil spirits and try to return. If they were let back in, the person could become worse off than before (see Matthew 12:44).

I explained that she could easily get rid of the evil spirits causing the problems and I was happy to help her do this, but that unless she gave her life to Jesus and chose to follow Him, then she may end up worse off if she let those things back! Without submitting her life to Jesus, she would have no spiritual authority to resist the demons in the future. So, I asked her what she wanted to do. She replied that she wanted to get rid of the evil spirits, ask God to forgive her and to give her life to Jesus. She wanted to know how to do this, and just as I'd done many times before, I began to help her pray.

For some reason, I generally like to pray with people standing up. Since I was also manning the check out in our shop at the time, I was already standing, so Angela slowly stood up next to me and this is what we did: I prayed and she repeated the words after me. She told God she was sorry for getting involved with reiki (she hadn't realized at the time that she was opening up to evil spirits). Then she asked Him to forgive her for going her own way and for all the sinful things she'd done in her life. She told the demon of fibromyalgia to leave in the name of Jesus. She breathed in the Holy Spirit and breathed out the spirit of fibromyalgia and pain. As it left, it made a sound like a train going through a tunnel. Then likewise the spirit of arthritis. As that left, she felt a strong pain in her neck and then it left. As the problem with her abdomen was identified, we realized that must be a demon too, as she felt what she described as claws ripping her abdomen. I suggested she tell the demon to cease causing pain and come out quickly, which it did. She then felt it move up through her body as it left through her mouth. The demon causing the migraines left with a sudden pain in her head and the fatigue exited with a long yawn!

Angela then invited Jesus to come into her life and asked the Holy Spirit to come and fill her. It was wonderful to be involved and see her being healed and set free by the power of Jesus. Her husband's eyes were almost out on stalks as he watched! So were a couple of customers who had come to the checkout to buy some of our gifts, but they seemed to take it all in their stride!

Angela began to bend and touch her toes – something she hadn't done in years. She then walked unaided and started to twirl around the shop, completely healed by Jesus. Her husband, Colin jumped up and hugged her with tears in his eyes. He said, 'thank you' to me over and over. He could hardly believe the change in his wife.

I then said to Angela, "You need to keep following Jesus. You now have the same Holy Spirit living in you who raised Jesus from the dead and who created the Universe. He's the Spirit of Jesus. If any of your previous symptoms try to come back, assume it's an evil spirit attempting to re-enter but don't let any of them in. Remember, an evil spirit can only have power in your life if you come into agreement with it. This is really important."

Angela was beside herself. She kept hugging me along with her husband. I took some video on my phone of her sharing what had just happened. It was wonderful. They both waved goodbye and thanked me again.

As with Angela, many people are suffering from illness that is simply caused by one or more evil spirits. ME, chronic fatigue, arthritis, fibromyalgia and migraines are all conditions that in my experience are usually caused by demons but easy to be set free from. In Angela's case, the evil spirits had entered through involvement in reiki as well as other things. But you may not have actively been involved with anything like that. However, I'm going to give you a couple of examples of other physical conditions that seem to be caused by evil spirits. It's important to be aware of what is happening in the spirit realm as that has a direct impact on the physical or natural realm.

The spirit of infirmity

Jesus met a woman who had been bent double for eighteen years (see Luke 13) and as He told the spirit of infirmity, a demon to leave, she was completely healed. A spirit of infirmity manifests in the body and can cause a hunched back, scoliosis, deformed limbs and bones and other conditions. Sometimes when a person has complications or a number of physical problems, it is caused by a spirit of infirmity.

Strokes

We used to run a café in our neighborhood and one day a man we knew came in at the same time as I was praying with a woman who'd suffered from a stroke six months previously. He was a mature Christian who knew about healing, however, at the same time I was telling the stroke symptoms to leave the woman, he began calling me from across the room, fairly insistently. As I went to see if he was okay, he told me he was having a stroke. I was surprized, but then realized the problem must be a spiritual one. I quickly deciphered that it must have been a demon that caused the stroke in the woman and as I told it to leave it looked for someone else to attack and it jumped on this man!

I quickly explained it was an evil spirit, he told it to leave and all the symptoms disappeared. Interesting to think that if we hadn't recognized what it was, he would probably have ended up in hospital suffering a stroke and all the subsequent life changing problems that would have caused. It really is important to be aware of what is happening in the spirit realm and to recognize that evil spirits can affect us if we simply accept them or come into agreement with them in any way.

A woodpecker story

My friend had come to my house for coffee one day and we'd been chatting away. Suddenly we both had the same symptoms at the same time: deafness, a migraine type headache, blurred vision and dizziness. Because we both felt the same thing at the same time, we recognized that it must have a spiritual cause. We began to pray and told any evil spirits to leave. The symptoms subsided apart from the headache. After my friend had left and the pain in my head wasn't leaving, I decided to get tough with the demon. I commanded it to leave me at the name of Jesus.

As soon as I had spoken this, I heard a loud bang and saw a bird drop dead outside the French windows the other side of the glass from where I was standing. Demons like to be in a body and as I told it to leave me, the nearest thing was a woodpecker. It was flying through our garden when the demon entered it, bashed into the upstairs window and broken its neck. It was on the deck outside the French windows, on its back with its legs in the air with its neck obviously broken and distorted.

The pain in my head had gone. I knew it had been an evil spirit, but I felt badly that it had killed the bird. I reckoned it was a spirit of death and possibly a curse. I decided to have a go at raising the bird from the dead. I wasn't sure if I needed to put my hand on the bird or even open the windows, but I thought the demon could probably hear me even through the closed French windows, as the spirit realm is not subject to glass doors! I told the spirit of death to leave and instantly the bird came back to life and flew away.

What I realized that day was that evil spirits will try and oppress us in any way they can and we need to recognize them for what they are and deal with them through the power of Jesus. The Bible describes it as being in a battle and that we're in a spiritual army. Warriors need to fight and our fight is not against flesh and blood (people), but against the powers of darkness (see Ephesians 6:12).

So, demons can cause migraine headaches, ear and sight problems, dizziness and death. In my experience, I've also noticed that evil spirits are directly related to many other conditions such as scoliosis, Obsessive Compulsive Disorder, Tourette syndrome, depression, arthritis, osteoporosis, cancer, fibromyalgia, ME, chronic fatigue, nerve pain, strokes, seizures, paralysis, being accident-prone, barrenness, addictions, heart failure, allergies, food intolerance and many more.

Deaf, blind and mute spirits

Jesus confronted many evil spirits that caused deafness, blindness and prevented people from speaking. As soon as He commanded those demons to leave, the people were completely healed and the onlookers amazed (see Matthew 9:33, Matthew 12:22 blind and mute, Mark 9:25 deaf and mute spirit, Luke 11:14 mute demon).

We ran a shop called 'Spirit' in the city of Chester and one day I chatted to a woman who was completely deaf in her left ear. She told me she had suddenly gone deaf two years previously when her husband had died. That seemed like a demon to me, so with my help, she asked God to forgive her for coming into agreement with that spirit of deafness and she told it to leave. She felt a whoosh as it left her ear and she instantly had 100% hearing restored.

Spirit of fear

Fear and anxiety can cause many illnesses and can kill you. Remember, an evil spirit can only have power in your life if you come into agreement with it in any way. I've known people who have worried so much about getting cancer or some other disease that they have ended up getting the very thing they worried about. There was a man named Job (pronounced Jobe) who had terrible calamities befall him. He lost everything; his family members died and he himself was very sick. Whilst talking to his friends he said, "What I feared has come upon me, what I dreaded has happened to me" (Job 3:25).

I've had people ask me about Job. "He was a God-fearing man and God let satan take away everything he had and make him sick, so what do you say to that?" I encourage them to read this verse in Job, where Job himself says, "The thing that I feared has come upon me". From this statement, we see that Job feared the worst. He must have come into agreement with the enemy's plan for his life; to steal, kill and destroy him and his family. The Bible says that satan went to God and asked permission to attack Job. God let him because Job was in agreement with satan. However, God would not permit Job to be killed. Perhaps Job wasn't in agreement with the devil's plans for that to happen, but what he did fear, satan was permitted to carry out.

If you can get this revelation about the power of agreement it could change your life. If we come into agreement with satan's plan for our lives, God has ordained that what we fear will be fulfilled. The Bible says, "The highest heavens belong to the Lord but the earth He has given to mankind" (Psalm 115:16). God has given us authority over what happens on the earth (see Genesis 1:28).

If we come into agreement with God's good plan, we will see that fulfilled in our lives as we keep following Jesus and submitting to Him and His ways. Jesus said, "Truly I tell you, whatever you bind on earth will be bound in heaven, and whatever you loose on earth will be loosed in heaven. Again, truly I tell you that if two of you on earth agree about anything they ask for, it will be done for them by my Father in heaven. For where two or three gather in my name, there am I with them" (Matthew 18:18-20).

This is powerful stuff and you really need to get this. Think about it. The enemy often works like this: An evil spirit comes to you but is very subtle. You come across news articles or social media posts about the likelihood of you developing a serious disease or you have a genetic history of something in your family, or you google symptoms that you are experiencing in your body. Your mind latches onto those 'facts' or possibilities and the evil spirit whispers to you that perhaps you have that disease or could do so in the future. You don't realize it's an evil spirit as it seems to be your own rational thoughts, seemingly real symptoms or even words from a person you respect. You read stories or hear doctor's advice to go for certain tests or to check yourself out regularly. Each time you do this, you think something may be found, and you begin to worry. You start to imagine the scenario in your head and begin to plan what you would do. While all this is happening, you are coming into agreement with that spirit of fear, that lying demon which is manifesting in your mind or your body.

We just read the Scripture that if two agree on earth about something, it will be done. You can bind something and stop it from happening and you can agree and cause it to happen. This can occur for good or for evil. Jesus said that He would be there when we come into agreement with Him, but the converse could also be true. Evil spirits are attracted when we come into agreement with the enemy. Not only can you empower an evil spirit in your life, but it can attract its cronies too, and you may find that one thing after another is coming against you.

So just as with Job, if you come into agreement with a demon that such and such may happen to you or you may have such and such in your mind or your body, that demon then has permission to make it happen. Because God has put earthly things under our authority, even God will not prevent that thing from happening if we've come into agreement with it. In His wisdom, God has made us extremely powerful in this way. You may be begging God to free you or heal you of something, but if you're the one that has agreed with the evil spirit that caused the problem in the first place, then you're the one who has to deal with it.

As with most things, you have a choice. You can choose to disagree with those thoughts or so called 'facts' and 'bind' them from having any power. You can choose to believe that God's word is true, that what Jesus did and said was not just for two thousand years ago, but He is the living word and is still powerful today. His power is available to you now.

Let's break off agreement right now with any evil spirit that has been working against you. I recommend you pray this out loud:

"Holy Spirit, please highlight to me the plans of the enemy against my life. Please show me now what they are and what I have said, done or thought that comes into agreement with those evil plans."

You may want to be quiet for a few moments and let the Holy Spirit reveal how the enemy plans to steal from you, destroy you and ultimately kill you. Write down anything that comes to mind, as well as how you have come into agreement with those things. Then you can say:

"Father God, please forgive me for coming into agreement with the enemy. I renounce the lie that I have… (or that I may get…) and I'm sorry that I have acted upon that lie by doing… or saying... and I command that demon and all of those symptoms to leave me now in the name of Jesus."

After saying this, breathe in deeply of the Holy Spirit and in your mind as you are doing this you can think, "Come and fill me Holy Spirit" and then breathe out any evil spirit that has been coming against you. If you feel something stuck in your throat, just give a cough, as evil spirits often come out through our mouths, particularly if connected to something we've agreed with verbally.

Keep breathing in the Holy Spirit and telling those evil spirits to leave you. Name and shame them! For example, "Spirit of fear, leave me now and don't come back." "Spirit of pain (or cancer or whatever) go now." "Evil spirit that is causing … go now and all the symptoms leave too." "I break off every generational curse that is coming against me and my children and grandchildren through the family line and I break its power by the blood of Jesus from me, my parents, grandparents and all the way back to Adam and Eve."

As you do this you may notice things leaving you. You may realize you're making a noise or coughing, yawning or belching a lot. You may get a pain in your body or dizziness as the evil spirit leaves or your symptoms may temporarily worsen, or the pain may move around your body. These are all signs that it's an evil spirit and it's on its way out, so don't give up. Keep insisting they leave until they have all gone, and feel free to tell them to leave without causing you pain. They have to do as you tell them through the power of Jesus.

Receive healing from Jesus for your mind, your emotions and your body. I release the healing power of Jesus for you. Go on, just receive it now. There's nothing stopping you being healed completely and instantly by Jesus. He loves you so much. He forgives you, He accepts you as you are; begin to believe it and receive it from Him. Be at peace and completely free. Where the Spirit of the Lord is, there is FREEDOM.

For further reading, I recommend my book 'How to be Free from Demons' where I go into more detail, share real life stories and help you get free and stay free.

CHAPTER NINE

Stay Safe: Counterfeit Healing Exposed

In the previous chapter, I told the story of Angela who became ill when she started to learn reiki. Over the years I've met many people who've been involved in reiki or other spiritual healing practices, but they all seem to have some sort of malady such as pain, sleep disorders, tiredness, headaches, depression or other mental or physical health problems. In addition, they often have issues with their relationships, finances and general wellbeing. I soon became aware that reiki and other practices were not just ineffective, but also potentially harmful.

At a recent workshop, a woman who had driven a few hundred miles to get there, told us that her right eye was blind. One of the other workshop attendees asked her if she was involved in New Age practices. It turned out that she was, and one day soon after she began practicing reiki, she'd actually seen a large dark shadow come towards her eye and had become instantly blind as a result. When we explained that it was an evil spirit that had caused the blindness, she readily agreed and wanted to know what to do about it. We helped her to pray, which she did out loud in front of the group. She asked Jesus to come into her life, she asked God to forgive her for going her own way, and the evil spirit was told to leave. It left at once and her eyesight was fully restored. Later that day, during the evening session, her husband and daughter also asked Jesus to come into their lives. That same day she was receiving words of knowledge from the Holy Spirit for others, she prayed for a woman who was instantly healed and then this new believer was also prophesying God's good plan for people's lives. What a difference turning away from New Age practices and turning to Jesus makes!

Over the years I've met many people who practice reiki and other healing methods that differ from the healing I offer through submitting my life to Jesus and being full of the Holy Spirit. The Bible says, "You will know them by their fruit." We want to bear good fruit, and the book of Galatians lists love, joy, peace and so on, as good fruit. I began to notice that virtually all of the people I met who practiced these other methods of healing, seemed to have some sort of ill health and other negative issues in their lives. So I decided to explore the origins of these now common practices and establish the source of the 'power' that is being used.

The truth about reiki

I discovered through many sites on the internet and chatting to those who have studied it, that reiki was started by a Japanese Buddhist as an alternative medicine in 1922. According to reiki practitioners, "Reiki is based on the idea that an unseen 'life force energy' flows through us and is what causes us to be alive." The internet states that "Reiki is spiritually guided life force energy." Nobody seems to know what this life force energy actually is, or from where it originates.

I discovered that reiki is a therapy often described as palm healing or hands-on-body healing in which a practitioner places hands lightly on or over a patient's body to facilitate the patient's process of healing. Reiki combines the Japanese and Chinese word-characters of "rei" (spiritual or supernatural) and "ki" (vital energy). It opens up both the practitioner and recipient spiritually and involves chakras and ancient healing symbols.

One time in Germany I was offered an aroma-therapy back massage by my hosts, as the wife had a visiting aromatherapist coming that morning. I agreed, and halfway through the massage, the therapist said to me, "You have a lot of powerful energy coming from you. I was going to do some reiki while I was massaging you but I couldn't do it, as the power from you was greater. What is that energy, I've never felt anything like it?" I explained to her that it was the Holy Spirit, the Spirit of Jesus and that I was full of His presence and His power and that Jesus was the highest power in the Universe.

She realized that the power she had been channelling through reiki was inferior power and was not from God. We chatted some more, then my hosts and I prayed with her. She could hardly remain standing due to the power of God and she then invited Jesus, the highest power, to come into her life. She asked God to forgive her for going her own way in life and for getting involved in reiki. She was amazed at how much better she felt and then went on to give up her reiki work and trained to become a nurse soon afterwards.

The fact is, many people who offer aromatherapy, massages and beauty treatments are trained to practice reiki. Even if you want nothing to do with reiki, if you decide to go for a massage, you may wish to tell the therapist beforehand not to do any reiki or realign your chakras and maybe skip the Indian Head Massage!

Lisa was a 'Reiki Master' and 'Pranic Healer', well known in our local area as someone who trained many people in reiki and other forms of healing. You can read Lisa's story in another of my books, but here is what she says about reiki:

"I got attuned to reiki nearly twenty years ago when I was eighteen. I was taught that it originates from Buddhist roots, mixed up with Christianity. In reiki when you place your hands on people, you are taught to channel the universal energy through you into other people to be healed.

I did level one and then when I became 'attuned' to the next level of reiki, I felt pushed out of the picture as I literally saw spirits coming around the bed of the person that was receiving the 'healing'. I watched as they did the work so I was actually just facilitating a 'healing' space. But it was demons that were coming. They didn't look like demons at the time: they looked like heavenly beings, angels of light. Sometimes they seemed intergalactic. There's a lot of emphasis on the lost world of Atlantis in the New Age so sometimes they'd look like Atlantean guides and they took on many different forms. The person would be lying face down and receiving from demonic beings as I stood there watching and instructing what was going on.

A lot of reiki practitioners are taught to protect themselves prior to conducting the healing session but in reality that can never really happen because you can't protect yourself from a demonic spirit that you have invited in. Inevitably you're sacrificing your own health to facilitate the 'healing' on that person. I was always quite physically tired from doing the reiki but I just had a big heart for people and wanted to see them get well.

Then I got involved with crystals. I would douse over the energy centers using a pendulum to check the chakras. Much of the teaching of the chakras is based on the Kabbalistic tree of life which is counterfeit, as the true tree of life is Jesus, but I didn't know that at the time. There is some power in the counterfeit, but it is limited and doesn't bring wholeness. It takes you on a roller coaster, feeling high during a reiki or pranic session and then low, just like any drug. But when Jesus comes into your life, you get that stability and have real joy on the inside.

One day when I was in the middle of a reiki treatment, I was watching who I thought was 'Jesus' doing the healing using universal energy and then the real Jesus came into the treatment room. He said, "Stop this now!" All of a sudden, the whole energy of the room completely shifted and there was this almighty power that came in like I'd never experienced before. True, perfect power and love."

Plugging into the wrong socket

Lisa goes on to say, *"I was plugging into the wrong socket! The power of the Holy Spirit does the work, I didn't need to have anything else channelling through me. Jesus is the healer. But I had to submit my life to Him and be full of His Holy Spirit for His power to flow through me.*

Why would you want to mix the counterfeit with the truth? Why settle for much less than the real deal, the highest power in the Universe who is Jesus, the Son of God? As soon as I found out I was not doing God's work and glorifying Him, I stopped the reiki and pranic healing. Now I have given my life to Jesus, I am experiencing so much more power and love for others."

Lisa was wanting to help people. Many of you reading this want to help people too and God is going to move through you powerfully so that you're healed and whole and so that you can reach out and help others to be whole in spirit, soul and body. But if you want to do this safely and tap into the highest power available to anyone, then it has to be through Jesus who is the only legal access point, the only safe way into the spirit realm. There are various ways into the spirit realm, but Jesus is the One through whom you will be kept safe. He is the only way into the Kingdom of Heaven, to Father God and to eternal life. Jesus said, "I am the door. Whoever enters by me will be saved (sozo = healed, made whole, set free and kept safe), and he or she can go in and out and find pasture, spiritual security. The thief comes to steal and kill and destroy, but I came that they may have and enjoy life in all its fullness" (see John 10:9,10).

Reflexology

Lisa also used to practice reflexology and she said this about it, *"We are taught that reflexology works on energy pathways, energy lines going from each foot upwards, crossing over at so-called 'chakras'. I was taught to manipulate the feet and that it would cause a healing response in the body, but again I discovered this as being counterfeit healing. A foot massage is a different story but any healing practice that is pointing to a source of spiritual power other than Jesus is a counterfeit."*

Acupuncture

Acupuncture is the ancient Chinese practice of inserting needles into certain points of the body to manipulate the flow of spiritual energy. In traditional Chinese medicine, acupuncture is linked to the belief that disease is caused by disruptions to the flow of this so-called spiritual energy in the body.

Again, anything or anyone that uses spiritual power that does not come from Jesus is dabbling in inferior, counterfeit and often dangerous methods. My feeling is, why do this instead of going directly to the ultimate source of power, Jesus? Through Him we receive healing and wholeness in every area of our lives and are kept safe in spirit, soul and body.

Psychic healing

Psychic healing is seen as an exchange of 'energy', but this energy is actually a spiritual force that is not the Holy Spirit. In fact it is often demonic but many people don't realize this and get involved because they want to be healed or want to heal others. Psychic healing involves one individual transferring this 'healing energy' to someone who needs it and the other person receives that 'healing energy'. Unfortunately, people who have been involved in this are actually transferring evil spirits from one to another but are not usually aware this is the case as demonic spirits often masquerade as beings of light or positive energy and auras. But then they wonder why they are not being healed or why the 'healing' doesn't result in peace, joy and love in their lives.

At the end of the day, don't mess around with your own 'energy' or receive other people's 'energies'. This is spiritual 'energy' we're talking about here. We need to protect ourselves and only receive from the Holy Spirit of Jesus who is God. We can receive His power for healing through other people. Psychic healing is counterfeit.

Yoga

Yoga originates from the Hindu religion. Corrina Craft was a Yoga Instructor for many years and as a Christian, thought she was safe from its spiritual influences. As an authority on the subject, in her YouTube videos she states: *"The active poses of yoga, the acrobatic poses, are the art of spiritual shape-shifting. The practitioner moulds her body into shapes resembling Hindu deities, avatars, heroes, sages and mythological creatures. The passive meditation poses are the body language of no self and no other, but cosmic being alone. You may be worshipping your God, but you are also inadvertently, unwittingly, performing ritual worship to beings from Hindu mythology and engaging in a physical philosophy. I got demonized teaching yoga even though I was reassigning it to Jesus. In the year 2010 I had two epic deliverances back to back. The first was the eviction of a demon of oriental medicine (see below) and the second was the eviction of a demon of yoga."* Corrina renounced the practice of oriental medicine, giving up ten years of work. After the demon of yoga manifested in her body and face when confronted, she researched and discovered that yoga is an occult practice. She immediately gave up yoga, asked God to forgive her and got rid of the demons associated with the practice. She now warns others of the dangers of yoga.

Oriental medicine

Corinna was also deeply involved in Oriental Medicine, including Shiatsu. She writes, *"Shiatsu is a*

Japanese form of massage that applies the principles and manipulative techniques of Traditional Chinese Medicine (TCM). I became adept at shiatsu and taught it for several years and wrote a textbook on the subject that was published by a prominent academic publisher. For about a decade, I immersed myself in the subject and became a subject matter expert.

I attended an equipping seminar on inner healing and deliverance taught by a Presbyterian minister. He had no knowledge of me whatsoever; he did not know I was a massage therapist, much less an expert in shiatsu. I volunteered for a public demonstration, and while he was briefly interviewing me, he got a word of knowledge, and the word was "shiatsu." I was puzzled but intrigued. Few people know about shiatsu because it is a niche speciality. "What's the matter with shiatsu?" I asked. He suggested it was demonic, but I was skeptical. After all, I had practiced shiatsu with a perfect sense of moral rectitude for a decade; I considered it a potent healing art, and I regarded massage as an extension of Christ's healing ministry through me. But the word of knowledge was so specific and so esoteric, only God could have given him such a word of knowledge. He had my curiosity and respect.

I doubt I would've been interested in exploring the possibility that a demon of shiatsu was obstructing my potential, if it hadn't been for the many dead ends in my career and my sense of frustration and futility in life. I was ready for revelation, but I was also realistic about the level of investment of my soul. I told him that I needed a dramatic manifestation because my mind could rationalize or discount a subtler one. He asked permission to invoke the demon, and I agreed, expecting nothing. At first nothing happened, yet after a while I felt an odd shifting and swirling force-field around my head. But that wasn't enough to convince me, for later I might attribute these sensations to insomnia, caffeine, low blood sugar, stress, or some other plausible cause, though I had never felt mentally queasy like that before. Suddenly, I began having heavy labored diaphragmatic breathing that sounded like a horse wheezing and that made my gut pump in and out. Then my right hand started slapping my thigh. Then my left foot started stomping on the ground. My eyes bulged, and a fierce expression settled on my face.

I was shocked! How could the demon hijack my autonomic and motor functions to such an extent? Clearly, another entity was living inside me, pushing the buttons and flipping the switches on my control panel!"

Corinna thankfully was delivered of this demon and has not been involved in Oriental Medicine since. She now warns others of the dangers of Yoga, Oriental Medicine and the like. She goes on to say, *"As a Taoist practice, Chinese medicine necessarily invited a demon to interpose itself between me and my client, whether I knew and wanted it or not... I was empowered by something more than the air I breathed and the energy I generated; I was empowered by a demon of oriental medicine."*

What to do next

If you've been involved with any type of counterfeit healing like reiki or yoga, it doesn't mean that you're a bad person. I expect you want to be well and healthy and you want other people to be well too. But you probably didn't realize that the power you've been subject to, was at best inferior and counterfeit, and at worst demonic. Well, now that you do, I recommend that you stop being involved with reiki or other types of healing that are not submitted to Jesus. You can pray the prayer with me below, and then start afresh, being full of the Holy Spirit and flowing in the miracle working power of Jesus and you won't look back!

We're going to tell those evil spirits to leave you in the name of Jesus, just like we did in the previous chapter so that you can give your life fully to God through His Son Jesus.

First let's speak to God:

"Holy Spirit, I invite you to come and manifest the presence of Jesus in the room. Father God, please forgive me for being involved in... (and if you have been a practitioner or teacher, then ask Him to forgive you for that too and for leading others along the wrong path). I renounce... (reiki, yoga or whatever you have been involved with) and every evil spirit associated with that and I command those evil spirits to leave me now in the name of Jesus. Holy Spirit come and fill me with your power and set me free."

Take a deep breath in of the Holy Spirit as He fills you with His power and then breathe or cough out all those evil spirits associated with counterfeit practices. Keep doing that until they are all gone. If you need help, ask a trusted Christian friend. What you need now is to be filled with the Holy Spirit so ask Him to do that more and more. You will soon notice a huge difference.

CHAPTER TEN

Be Healed!

You may have already received your healing whilst reading through this book as you gain revelation and encounter the power of Jesus, but for those of you not yet healed, this is for you. At the end of this chapter I'm going to pray with you for healing. But first I want to tell you something else that may help you.

One time I was speaking at a conference in North Wales. The original speaker had cancelled and at the last minute I got a phone call asking me to help out by being the key speaker instead. I was pleased to accept, although I realized that everyone who'd signed up to the conference was expecting an international prophet and I was just the substitute. However, I knew it was right for me to be there. I taught on the Kingdom of Heaven and demonstrated God's power. But as I often do, I invited other people to have a go at doing the miracles.

During one session, I told the story of 'Terry Fingers'. You may have read about Terry in my first book, 'A Diary of Miracles Part 1'. Terry had pieces of glass embedded in his fingertips for a number of years and when I told all glass to come out of his body at the name of Jesus, it all came out that night, including glass in his foot that he hadn't known about.

After sharing this story in Wales, I invited anyone to come to the front who had anything like glass in their body. A woman called Tracy came out. She showed me a large lump under the skin on a finger of her right hand and told me it had been there for twenty-six years! But that wasn't her main problem: her lower arm and right hand were twisted inwards like a claw. She explained that she'd contracted 'cat scratch disease' with complications, had been hospitalized for eleven days, had surgery and almost had to have her arm amputated due to cellulitis and an abscess. As a result her fingers were numb, she said she couldn't hold a cup and I could see a long scar on the back of her hand from the surgery. She was unable to work anymore and it was obvious to all that her hand and arm were severely deformed.

I asked the audience, "Who has never done a miracle before but would like to do one now?" A young boy, four years of age, ran up to the front, obviously excited and wanting to have a go. He put his finger on Tracy's hand and with some help, told the glass to disappear through the power of Jesus. He took his little hand away, and to Tracy's surprise, the large lump had disappeared! She pressed the area with her other hand and realized not only had the glass gone after twenty-six years, but she had feeling in her deformed hand.

I remembered reading in Mark chapter three, how Jesus had told a man with a withered hand to "stretch out your hand" and it was healed, so I said the same to Tracy. She stretched it out and the withered, claw-like hand became normal as we all watched on in amazement. I love Jesus! I took some video the following day as Tracy, accompanied by the boy's mother, described how her life had transformed since her healing just 24 hours before. Not only that, but the long scar on her hand from the surgery had almost disappeared by the following day and the next time I saw her it had gone completely. That day she had been back to work, doing everything she hadn't been able to do since the surgery. Even gold dust appeared supernaturally as she was telling people what Jesus had done.

You can watch this video and others mentioned in this book on the playlist 'How to be healed' on my website www.alisscresswell.com.

Sometimes Jesus would ask the person who wanted to be healed to do something in order for them to receive their healing. It is so important to obey the Holy Spirit. Jesus paid the price for your sin and your healing but it's up to you whether you receive that for yourself. Just like when you receive forgiveness for your sins, you receive it by faith, the same is true of healing. I've prayed for atheists and they've been healed. You don't need much faith, but simply agreeing to be prayed for or submitting to Jesus may be all it takes for you to receive your miracle.

A woman I met in our café was dramatically healed by Jesus. Sometime later she brought a relative of hers into the café and asked if Jesus would heal her too. The younger woman told me she'd suffered an accident at work and had to have surgery on her back, but the doctors had told her she would have permanent problems as a result. She had been through a lengthy process of suing her previous employer and was hoping to receive a large amount of money in damages and ongoing financial support as well as a brand new car and house rent free from the government due to her being unable to work.

She was in a lot of pain and I asked her if she wanted to be healed. She did, however, she told me she was reluctant to lose all the benefits and the large amount of compensation money that would come in a few months' time. I told her she had to decide. One or the other. Thankfully, after thinking it all through, she made the wise decision to choose healing from Jesus and give up the disability benefits and the court case. She was immediately healed.

You too may need to make a decision like that. You may need to give up government benefits, a house, car, disability income, special parking spaces, reliance on others, carers and other support. Once you've been healed, you may need to get a job. But as you make the choice to stop relying on those things, and instead trust God for your health, your finances and your support, then God will honor that and you will begin to live a life of freedom, health, joy and peace. Assistance, if we need it, can be a blessing, but not if it becomes an obstacle to our healing. We need to be honest with ourselves about this. So if that's you, then maybe take some time now to make those decisions. Begin to imagine yourself completely well, able to work, enjoying life, with healthy relationships, and helping others. What an inspiration you will be and a role model for others to follow!

I love the story in the Bible where Peter's mother-in-law was sick and in bed with a fever. Jesus comes in, touches her hand, the fever instantly leaves her and so she gets up and begins waiting on them. When you're healed you can do everything you used to do before you were sick without even the need to convalesce (see Matthew 8:15).

Tracy and the man with the withered hand in the Bible both stretched out their hands before they were healed. In a similar way, you may need to do something to receive your miracle too. Why not pray this prayer out loud with me, expect a miracle and then step out in faith and try doing something you couldn't do before? Just the act of bending over, taking out your hearing aids, getting up from your wheelchair or some other act of faith like stretching out your deformed hand may be the key you need.

Pray this out loud:

"I invite the healing presence of Jesus to come now. Thank you Jesus that you took all my pain and diseases when you went to the cross. I ask you to forgive me for relying on certain things in my life such as... and I choose to trust you. I command ... to leave my body (or my mind or emotions) in the name of Jesus. Please come Holy Spirit with your healing power. I receive the healing now, in the name of Jesus, Amen."

Now do that thing that you couldn't do before and see how Jesus has healed you!

Expect complete healing. Get firm with the problem, tell it to go and keep testing it out until it has completely gone. Be persistent and insistent and don't let it stay any longer. It has no right to be there, it's like a trespasser or a squatter and the only right it has to remain is if you come into agreement with it.

I agree with you for your healing. We come into agreement with Heaven and release the power of Jesus into your life: your mind, your body, your soul. Receive it now, by faith. Freedom and healing are a gift from God for you, right now. Begin to thank Him for what He has done and for what He is doing in your life. Just like He did for Tracy and the man with the withered hand, and all the other miracles you've heard about, He wants to do for you. It doesn't matter how good or bad a person you think you are. You don't need to stay in pain or with any affliction or sickness or disease. This is a new day. Your new life can start right now.

Keep trusting God to restore you completely. Thank Him for what He has already done and what He is going to do and I'm going to share another remarkable story with you.

One day a guy came into the shop we used to run, to buy a present for his wife's birthday. I asked him why he limped and he told me that he'd had a car accident thirty years previously, and had almost died. He had three crushed vertebrae which were pressing on his spinal cord, he had sciatica and had been in constant pain for the past thirty years. He had also lost four inches in height due to the accident and was told he would be in a wheelchair soon. He had bruising on the brain which caused epilepsy, a reconstructed jaw, he'd lost all his teeth, had a new top palate and often woke up with a bleeding mouth, numb arms and legs. Undeterred, I told him that Jesus could heal him. He seemed a bit unsure but let me pray for him. We were standing in the middle of the shop with other customers browsing the gifts.

I began to pray and felt the power of God strongly. He was unable to speak due to the power he felt going through his body. My husband Rob had to run and catch him as he was falling under the power of Jesus. I asked him how he felt and he was so shocked that he began to cry. He was hardly able to speak he was so overcome, but was able to tell us that this was the first time in thirty years that he could feel no pain. He sat down and cried. Before we had prayed I watched him try to get up out of his seat and it took him a while due to all the pain, but after we prayed I asked him to stand up again and he literally jumped up.

He told me that each time he'd sat for a while, like when he went to the movies, it would take about twenty minutes to get up out of his seat, but this time he stood up it took him seconds. He told us that he was taller too. He certainly looked like he had grown a few inches. His mouth became numb as we prayed for a reconstruction of his jaw. He felt heat in it. He then told us that his hands had been shaking constantly since the accident but now they were still. He said he felt giddy, he was stunned and was still crying as the realization that he could be healed dawned on him. He stayed in the shop for a long time that day and only left because he had to go back to work. Before he left he gave his life to Jesus.

Now test out your body again. How are you doing? I would love to hear from you. If you can, take some video footage of yourself before and after, or get a friend to do it for you. As soon as you know you are healed, write me a message with all the details and I'd love to see your video if you took one. My contact information is at the back of this book.

CHAPTER ELEVEN

Practical Steps to Staying Healed

Remember I told you about Angela who came into our shop and was set free from demons and completely healed? At the time, I'd told her: "You need to keep following Jesus. You now have the same Holy Spirit living in you who raised Jesus from the dead and who created the Universe. He's the Spirit of Jesus. If any of your previous symptoms try to come back, treat them like evil spirits and don't let them in. Remember, an evil spirit can only have power in your life if you come into agreement with it. This is really important."

Imagine my surprise, when a few weeks later Angela came back into our shop, this time shuffling in and leaning on a walking frame. She could hardly walk and was bent over. Her face was contorted with pain. Her husband helped her in and shook his head. He told me that for a few weeks it was as though he had a new wife. He was no longer her carer and she was just like a 'normal' person, completely pain free. Angela joined in, "The pain suddenly came back and was so bad I went to my doctor again." She'd actually come off all her medication for a few weeks after she'd been healed but now was on double the original dose of painkillers.

I asked her if she remembered to do what I'd told her after her healing. She couldn't remember anything I'd said as she'd been so overwhelmed, so I explained it to her again. She realized that she'd let the evil spirits back in by coming into agreement with them, the pain had intensified and she was actually worse than before. She felt awful. She cried and said she was sorry, and asked if it was too late to do anything now. I comforted her with the fact that all she needed to do was tell God she was sorry for coming into agreement with the enemy and to tell those cheeky demons to leave. So she did. They left, she was completely healed and this time she knew what she must do to stay healed. She told me she would go back to her doctor and come off all medication and that if any symptoms tried to return, she'd tell them to leave and would not come into agreement in any way. Thankfully, this time she knew what she must do.

So, what made the difference? Why did Angela not keep her healing for more than a few weeks the first time she was healed? What changed the second time I saw her?

Anyone can be healed through the power of Jesus, whether they believe in Him or not. As I've already mentioned, I've seen a number of atheists instantly healed and hundreds of others have been healed and remain healed without following Jesus. However, living in divine health is something different. If you want to stay healthy with the power to overcome sickness and evil spirits in your life and the lives of others, you need to submit your life to Jesus and follow Him.

In the Bible, Jesus states that when an evil spirit leaves a person, it goes through dry places looking for rest and not finding any, may return. If it finds the same person 'like a house swept clean', it may invite other evil spirits to enter 'the house' together. The resulting condition of that person could therefore be worse than before (see Matthew 12:43-45).

Sickness is often caused by an evil spirit and when that spirit is driven out and you are healed, it may try and come back in sometime later. When you submit your life to Jesus Christ and invite Him into your life, He will come in through the power of the Holy Spirit and will not leave you. If an evil spirit bringing those original symptoms (or any others for that matter), tries to come against you in the future, you have the resident power of Jesus, the Holy Spirit in you and can therefore prevent the enemy from having any power over you. You need the revelation of what that means, of just how powerful Jesus is and you can then block any enemy advances against your mind, soul and body through His power and not let any evil spirits in.

The only way an evil spirit can have power in your life is if you come into agreement with it in any way. In my book 'How to be Free from Demons', I go into this in more detail, but for now it is important that you know what to do and put it into action.

You need to get the balance right though. Don't automatically assume the sickness will try and come back. Remember the power of agreement and what may happen if you assume the worst. Expect to stay healed. Most people we pray for are healed immediately and remain healed. But occasionally the problem can try and come back a few days or weeks later. It is easy to succumb to the pain or symptoms, particularly if you have been used to the illness for a long time. But it is important to stand your ground. Speak to the symptoms or the pain out loud and tell it to "Leave now in the name of Jesus". Treat it as an evil spirit; something that is illegal and has no right to try and reside in your body. When Jesus went to the cross He took all sickness and pain, He paid the price, it was laid on His body so you don't need to carry it too. The sickness is a lie of the enemy so rebuke it. You may need to do this a few times before it stops pestering you but please do not give up or accept the illness back.

Remember, God does not allow you to be sick in order to glorify Him any more than He would want you to sin. It is a lie of the enemy. You will find if you take a stand and refuse to give in to the symptoms, it will have to leave. However, if you come into agreement with the symptoms in any way, you will find that the illness settles back and can be more difficult to shift the next time.

Becoming part of God's family

When you recognize that Jesus died on the cross and took all your sin and diseases, and you believe He is the Son of God, you then need to make a decision to follow Him. When you choose to give over the control of your life to Him and ask Him to come into your life, He will do that. A wonderful eternal relationship with God begins right at that moment. The Bible says that you actually become a brand new creation! You are taken out of darkness and are brought into light, into God's Kingdom and His Family. God becomes your Father and other Christians become your brothers and sisters. God says, "I will never leave you nor abandon you" (Hebrews 13:5). God is a faithful Father.

Receive peace, freedom and fulfillment in your life

To begin this new life, you can start by praying the following prayer out loud:

"Father God, I thank you for sending your Son Jesus to die on the cross for me. Thank you that He paid the price for all my sin and my illnesses and addictions and fear. Thank you that Jesus rose again and overcame all the power of satan in my life. Please help me to turn away from all that is negative in my life. I ask you to forgive me for the things I have done that are wrong, particularly... (tell God particular things that come to mind, things you regret or cause you to feel guilt or shame).

Thank you that I am forgiven! Jesus, I invite you to come into my life through the power of your Holy Spirit. I renounce satan in my life and declare that I am no longer in the Kingdom of darkness, but I have a new life in Jesus and I am now in God's family. I break the power of satan in my life through the blood of Jesus that was poured out for me at the cross. Father God, please fill me with your power and love, by your Holy Spirit. In the name of Jesus, Amen."

I have written this prayer and others in a small booklet which is perfect for anyone wanting to know more about Jesus. It explains who He is, what He accomplished on the cross and how you can know Him. Once you have prayed this prayer, you are now a new creation, and Jesus lives on the inside of you.

Power of Communion

A good thing to practice regularly is Communion. There is great power in the act of Communion and by faith it can bring health to your body. You can take Communion on your own or with friends, in your home or at church. You don't need anything special to do this, but the act of Communion or 'The Lord's Supper' is very powerful and many people find they are healed as they participate.

I will explain the reason for this. The night before His betrayal and subsequent death and resurrection, Jesus spent the evening with His close friends. It was the time of a Jewish Festival called the 'Passover'. As they were eating the Passover meal, Jesus took the bread they were eating, broke it and shared it with His friends saying, "This bread is my body given for you. Do this to remember me". Then He took a cup of wine, shared it amongst them and said, "This cup is the new covenant in my blood which is poured out for you" (see Luke 22).

Jesus was asking His friends and followers to share in what we now call 'Holy Communion' or 'The Lord's Supper'. The reason it is so powerful when we do this is because when we take the bread and remember what Jesus accomplished on the cross, we are declaring that Jesus' health and life flows in our bodies. When we drink from the cup in this way and are thankful for Jesus, we are declaring that we have been bought with a price, washed clean and forgiven. Jesus' blood gives us right standing before God and enables us to go boldly into His presence (see Hebrews 4:16).

Would you like to take Communion now? Jesus used bread and wine as that's what was at His table, but many people prefer crackers and juice, or whatever else is to hand. We don't want to make this into some sort of ritual, but we do want our hearts to be right before God. It's wonderful when we share the bread and the cup with friends and is a great thing to do whilst eating a meal with friends who love Jesus.

You may not have done this before, but we can do so now if you are able to find something to drink and something to eat. First of all, take the bread (or whatever is to hand) and say something like this:

"Thank you Jesus that you died in my place. Thank you that you went to the cross and willingly laid down your life for me. I recognize that your body was broken for me and all my pain, sorrow and sickness was laid on you as you went to the cross." You may wish to imagine yourself placing all these things afflicting your body, your mind and emotions onto Jesus and letting Him carry them to the cross for you. "By your wounds I have been healed."

Now eat the bread. Then take the cup (or can or water bottle) and say something like this:

"Thank you Jesus that your blood was poured out for my sins. I receive your forgiveness. You bought me with a great price. I am washed clean, I have a fresh start, I am a new person now because of your love for me. Your blood protects me and cleanses me from all sin. Thank you for your blood of the new Covenant. I receive your forgiveness and your life." Now drink from the cup.

You can do this as often as you like. Some people do it every day, others just now and again. It is more powerful than you know. There is power in the blood of Jesus. And you may find as you do this, that suddenly you are well. Simply believe.

Water baptism

Another powerful act of obedience to God is baptism in water. The original word for baptism means 'to be submerged'. I know people who have been healed physically and others who have been set free from addictions or other negative traits as they go under the waters of baptism. My husband Rob in his book, 'The Believer's Guide to Survival' (formerly 'What Next Jesus?') writes:

"Believer's Baptism in water is a Christian act that symbolises personal repentance (a turning away from sin) and belief in Jesus Christ as saviour. I call it 'Believer's Baptism' because, unlike the christening of a baby, it requires that the individual understands the gospel message and confesses and acts upon it for themselves. Immersion in water is a symbol of dying with Christ, and emergence from the water a symbol of being raised with Him to eternal life… Baptism is an outward expression of what has happened to you on the inside and a public identification with Christ."

A healthy lifestyle

Following the way of love through Jesus, taking a stand against evil spirits and any symptoms, being baptized and participating in Communion regularly can all help you to stay healed. However, it's important not to forget that your lifestyle - your food, drink and exercise all have an important part to play.

My friend Beth was diagnosed with cancer two years ago. She was subsequently healed through the supernatural power of Jesus and by completely changing her lifestyle and eating natural food and not applying or consuming toxins. Here's what she says:

"My husband and I had raised our family and lived in Arizona in the South West of the USA for many years. Over the course of two months we felt the Lord was giving us explicit directions to sell everything and pack the car with only the necessities and head to the South East of the US. Given the fact that we were giving up everything; house, job, etc, I decided to get all my doctor's visits in before we left. Three days before we were scheduled to leave, I was informed by my doctor that I had breast cancer.

After the turmoil of hearing the news and having an emergency appointment to assess the situation, we collected ourselves and prayed to ask the Lord what to do. We both had peace that God would not have prepared us for this journey, just to leave us before we set out. We ended up living in Atlanta for a few months and I decided to fly back to Phoenix to have a quick lumpectomy. However, the test came back that I now had cancer in my lymph nodes and the doctor upgraded the diagnosis and changed the treatment plan to include full radiation and chemotherapy as well as a possible mastectomy.

Before calling my husband in Atlanta with the devastating news, he had already heard the Lord say in prayer that I was healed and to come back. We knew the Lord was not wanting us to do anything at that moment except pray. Before returning to Atlanta, the Lord spoke to us again and confirmed it many times that we were to now head south to Hilton Head Island, SC. This is where the Lord started to speak to us about Him not just healing the cancer, but healing the cause of it. We started to really seek His wisdom on lifestyle choices. We knew of natural healing, but this was different; He had put a strong desire in our hearts to learn how to live a healthy lifestyle. We learned about food and all the things that God has given us for natural healing and to remain healthy, but I was still looking into radiation, chemotherapy and lining up doctors on the Island just in case we decided to go down that route. However, I realized later that by doing this, I was agreeing with the enemy by allowing my fear of dying and recent life changes to influence my decisions.

We learned so much in such a short amount of time. We knew the Lord had brought us to the understanding of natural healing and immediately put it into action. We cut out many of the unhealthy foods we had been eating. God gave us the strength and understanding to change our lifestyle and as a result, not only was the cancer healed but my husband and I even lost 100 pounds between us! It was amazing how the Holy Spirit sent people with wisdom in all different areas and even had strangers come up to me and say they saw healing all over me! God is so good to send us affirmations along the journey. Slowly the fear and confusion that satan wanted me to have, turned into the power and strength of my almighty God. It was a long year, but by the end of it I felt like I had the peace of knowing that my name is already written in the book of life. My time to go home is already known by God and I was not going home any sooner than already written. Satan and his fearful conniving thoughts cannot have my power. My DNA is that of Jesus Christ! I then had more tests done which showed I was healed of cancer."

It is so important to look after yourself by eating healthy food, incorporating regular exercise into your routine and not eating more calories than your body is burning. There are many books on the subject so I don't need to go into the details here. Suffice to say, we need to make wise choices for the health of our mind, body and soul. It isn't easy when we'd rather stay in bed a little longer, drive rather than walk and eat delicious but unhealthy food, but we should be able to strike a balance and enjoy life as well as living healthily.

CHAPTER TWELVE

Share What You Have Learned With Others

What I am teaching you in this book is extremely powerful and is very good news. Too good, in fact, to keep to yourself. What you have been learning has the power to transform your world if you put it into practice, and people will begin to ask what has happened to you. They'll want to know your secret as they see your health and lifestyle improve and it's important that you share with them what God has shown you and done for you.

The best way is to simply tell your friends, family and colleagues how your life has changed through the power of Jesus and then demonstrate to them the power of the good news of the Kingdom of God. Share with them how God has impacted your life and then demonstrate His love and power to them tangibly. I love doing this, especially when I meet someone who says they're an Atheist or who thinks it's just 'mind over matter'.

Miracles in a pub

I was staying at a pub in South Wales one weekend as I was speaking at a workshop nearby and booked into the pub for B&B. Saturday afternoon I had arranged to record a radio interview with a local station. The radio show host came to the pub and we recorded the interview. Towards the end of the program, I suggested we go outside and find some people who needed healing. I spotted a young woman who had the same handbag as me, so I thought that would be a good place to start!

I approached the woman as the DJ carried the recording equipment behind me. We explained to her and her friends that we were making a radio show and we thought it would be good to have some 'live' healings. I asked if the woman had anything wrong with her and it turned out she had pelvic problems since birth and was about to have surgery. We offered to pray, and she felt something happening. I instructed her to walk up and down and test out the healing, so she did and said the pain had gone and she felt like it was normal. We explained that it was due to the healing power of Jesus and told her about Him.

We then moved back into the pub and got chatting to the owner who was behind the bar. He had trouble with his legs and back, so we prayed and the DJ recorded him saying how the pain had left and we watched him walk up and down some steps with no problem.

A couple of hours after this, I was up in my B&B room praying about the evening meeting, when I sensed the Holy Spirit tell me to go downstairs and sit outside the back door of the pub. I was obedient and walked downstairs. I noticed a pub table with benches so I sat at that. A couple of minutes later, two workmen appeared from inside the pub carrying pints of beer. They'd come outside to have a cigarette. I could overhear their conversation as they were discussing quite loudly the fact that some strange miracles had been happening earlier in the day and everyone was talking about it.

I got up and began to tell them how I was there when the miracles happened and it was the power of Jesus that had healed the people. One of the workmen said, "Oh it's all in yer head" and tried to explain the miracles away, telling me and his friend that the power of the mind could work wonders. I agreed that taking control over your own thoughts was a good idea, but that mind over matter was unable to help cure people of terminal illnesses or conditions such as Multiple Sclerosis that I had seen healed by the power of Jesus.

I asked the men if either of them had any pain or physical conditions and both told me they had. One of the guys had a problem with his back. He let me put my hand on his shoulder and as I released the power of Jesus he began to sway and exclaimed that something good was happening. He then showed me his hand – the scaphoid bone on the back of his hand was broken and it was sticking right out, you could see it when he held his hand up. He had damaged it three years previously and needed an operation for metal pins to be inserted into it. He said it would require three months off work. I said, "I'm going to demonstrate to you now that God is real, that He loves you. When He heals you, it'll prove the power of Jesus and the fact that it's not just 'in your head'!" He replied, "Go on then!"

So I put my finger on top of his hand. Not only was the bone protruding and in the wrong place, but I could feel it under my finger. I released the power of Jesus and spoke to the bones. I told all the bones to move around and get into the right place, and anything damaged to be made completely whole.

The guy started laughing as he felt the bones in his hand move when I took my finger away, and we watched as the bone literally moved back into the correct position. Both he and his friend were freaking out and could hardly believe it. He kept saying, "That's nuts that is. That's nuts. I'm not joking, that's really moved back into place." You can watch this video and others mentioned in this book on the playlist 'How to be healed' on my website www.alisscresswell.com.

His friend asked me if I could do something with his ankle. He said he'd broken it twice and it was messed up. So I did the same: I released the power of Jesus when I put my hand near his ankle and told the bones to be made whole and to move into the right place, and for strength to come back into his ankle. He said he could feel it tingling and said, "I think you've sorted it right out!"

Jesus empowers others to heal

When He walked the earth, Jesus healed everyone who came to Him. We see in the Scriptures that not only did Jesus heal people, but He told His followers that they could heal others too. Let's look at those verses now.

Matthew 10:1 records that "Jesus called his twelve disciples to him and gave them authority to drive out impure spirits and to heal every disease and sickness."

Jesus also sent out many more of His followers to release healing and freedom too. In Luke chapter ten we read how he appointed seventy two to go and declare that the Kingdom of God had come, and to heal the sick and drive out demons. We read how these newly appointed followers of Jesus came back excitedly sharing their stories of miracle working power and how even the demons had to obey them through the name of Jesus.

The miracles that Jesus did were not just to prove His divinity, but to fulfil His commission - the will of God. Jesus then commissioned the twelve disciples to heal, He commissioned the seventy two. His commission was given to all who believe. He commissioned the church: "And the prayer offered in faith will make the sick person well; the Lord will raise them up. If they have sinned, they will be forgiven" (James 5:14,15). These commissions still stand.

After Jesus ascended to heaven, His followers waited to be 'clothed with power from on high' by the Holy Spirit (see Acts 1 and 2). Let's look at some of the extraordinary miracles they subsequently performed after being empowered by the Spirit of Jesus:

"When the crowds heard Philip and saw the signs he performed, they all paid close attention to what he said. For with shrieks, impure spirits came out of many, and many who were paralyzed or lame were healed. So there was great joy in that city" (Acts 8:6-8).

"One day Peter and John were going up to the temple at the time of prayer — at three in the afternoon. Now a man who was lame from birth was being carried to the temple gate called Beautiful, where he was put every day to beg from those going into the temple courts. When he saw Peter and John about to enter, he asked them for money. Peter looked straight at him, as did John. Then Peter said, "Look at us!" So the man gave them his attention, expecting to get something from them. Then Peter said, "Silver or gold I do not have, but what I do have I give you. In the name of Jesus Christ of Nazareth, walk." Taking him by the right hand, he helped him up, and instantly the man's feet and ankles became strong. He jumped to his feet and began to walk. Then he went with them into the temple courts, walking and jumping, and praising God" (Acts 3:1-8).

Authority to move in power through Jesus

Well, we've just seen that Jesus healed every sick person who came to Him. We've looked at Scriptures in the Bible showing that He commissioned his twelve disciples and empowered seventy two others to heal the sick too, and then His followers continued to heal the sick after Jesus ascended to heaven and they were baptized with the Holy Spirit. Now we will see that Jesus gives His power through the Holy Spirit, and authority to use that power, to everyone who follows Him to do the same. This means you and I, in this day and age. Healing is for us. Let's check out what He said.

"Whoever believes and is baptized will be saved, but whoever does not believe will be condemned. And these signs will accompany those who believe: In my name they will drive out demons... they will place their hands on sick people, and they will get well" (Mark 16:16-18).

Here is another amazing verse. When I first heard someone preach from it years ago, I had to look it up in my Bible and read it a few times before I was convinced that Jesus really did say it. He was talking about miracles at the time. "I tell you the truth, anyone who has faith in me will do what I have been doing. He will do even greater things than these, because I am going to the Father. And I will do whatever you ask in my name, so that the Son may bring glory to the Father. You may ask me for anything in my name and

I will do it" (John 14:12-14). It's almost too good to be true. But it is true.

Read that verse a few times and drink it in. Meditate on it and learn it. It could change your life and the lives of your loved ones. In this passage, as Jesus is talking about miracles, He states that we can do the same works He did, and even greater! So, if you believe that Jesus is the Son of God and you have asked Him to come into your life, you can do the things He did. If your body needs healing, you can release healing for yourself, or if you come across someone who is ill or in pain, you can release healing for them, through the power of Jesus the Son of God.

Making a place for healing

Healings broke out when we opened our café in Blacon, a suburb of Chester, UK in 2009. You can read the stories in my books, 'A Diary of Miracles' Part I and II. It began with many healings of broken bones, but there have been all manner of miracles including multiple sclerosis, deafness, blindness, sciatica, spine problems, torn ligaments, diabetes, arthritis, strokes, cancer and many other diseases, all healed by the power of Jesus. We opened a shop called 'Spirit' in Chester city centre one year later and the same thing happened in there from the day we opened. Now miracles happen everywhere we go and we train and activate others to do the same through our workshops, home parties, videos and online training.

Give it a go!

Get yourself a Bible or a Bible app and study the Word of God and what it says about healing. Learn some of the verses I've quoted by memory. Step out in faith and pray for the sick. I tend not to pray for God to heal someone, but rather I take authority over the sickness or demon and command it to leave in the name of Jesus. Sometimes I speak to it two or three times before it goes, but it usually takes less than a minute or two. Practice praying whilst going about your usual routine: in the supermarket, at work, at the school gate, in a neighbor's drive or wherever. You will find that you don't have time to pray a long prayer.

Release the power of Jesus as you pray. Often you will feel power coming out of your hands (that is the anointing) or waves of the Holy Spirit as He ministers to the person. Be aware of any sensations you may feel in your body as they could be words of knowledge helping you discern what a person's problem is. Share them with the person as the Holy Spirit leads.

Here's one last story I want to share with you to show you that it isn't just me who can do miracles but anyone who follows Jesus can see the sick get well:

One day a woman with cancer went into our shop, Spirit, in Chester. She was about to undergo surgery to have a large cancerous tumor the size of an egg removed from the back of her neck. The tumor was pressing on nerves and tissue which meant her arm was numb and she was unable to lift or move her arm very far. Her husband was a surgeon and even though she was a Christian, she thought she had no option but to have surgery and chemotherapy.

She came into our shop simply for prayer for God's peace as she was quite anxious about the surgery. I wasn't in the shop that day, but she met two of our volunteers, Wendy and Joy. She told them the problem and asked if they'd pray for peace about the operation and that it would go well. They said they were happy to pray for God's peace to come, but how about they release the power of Jesus for complete healing? She agreed, so they began to pray and they told the cancerous tumor to leave her body. As they were praying, the woman found that feeling had come back to her arm. She then raised it up high with no problem, bent her elbow and went to put her hand on the back of her neck to touch the tumor. But as she did so, she realized that the whole egg-sized tumor had completely disappeared. She couldn't believe it, but it had really gone. Just like that. She went home to show her husband and went back to the hospital to meet up with the surgeon who was treating her. After tests, she was told the cancer had all gone. That's my Jesus and if He will do it for her, He'll do it for you. Be healed, in the name of Jesus!

I have put together some of my favorite verses from the Bible for you. Read these and take them as promises for you and your loved ones:

"For Christ died for sins once for all, the righteous for the unrighteous, to bring you to God. Jesus humbled himself and became obedient to death - even death on a cross. Therefore God exalted him to the highest place and gave him the name that is above every name, that at the name of Jesus every knee should bow, in heaven and on earth and under the earth. Having disarmed the powers and authorities, he made a public spectacle of them, triumphing over them by the cross. He says, 'I am the Living One; I was dead, and behold I am alive for ever and ever! And I hold the keys of death and hell'. You are saved by the resurrection of Jesus Christ, who has gone into heaven and is at God's right hand - with angels, authorities and powers in submission to Him, and by His wounds you have been healed. For in Christ all the fulness of the Deity lives in bodily form, and you have been given fulness in Christ, who is the Head over every power and authority. Jesus says, 'All authority in heaven and on earth has been given to me. Therefore, go into all the world and preach the good news to all creation. And these signs will accompany you who believe: In my name you will drive out demons, you will place your hands on sick people and they will get well'."*

Let me know how you get on. Be sure to keep a record of what happens in your own life and others whom you share this good news with. I'd love to receive your reports and your 'before and after' doctor's notes and scans, videos, photographs and messages.

*For Bible references for this passage, go to my website www.AlissCresswell.com

Also if you have chosen to follow Jesus whilst reading this book, please do tell me. You can contact me through my website and social media. Details are on the following pages. All glory goes to Jesus for what He has done for us. Jesus is Lord and I love Him.

www.AlissCresswell.com

If you have been impacted by this book, I would love to hear about your experience! Go to my website contact form and send me a message.

Or email: contact@AlissCresswell.com

Follow Aliss on:

Facebook, Twitter, Instagram, YouTube & iTunes Podcast

More Resources from
Rob & Aliss Cresswell
Books, CDs & DVDs

MY VIDEO DIARY

MY ITINERARY

MY BLOG

MY RESOURCES

PRAY WITH ME

CONTACT ME

Visit my website

www.AlissCresswell.com

and watch the 'How to Be Healed' videos featured in this book.